nickelodeon™

降击神通

AVATAR

THE LAST AIRBENDER™

Created by
Bryan Konietzko
Michael Dante DiMartino

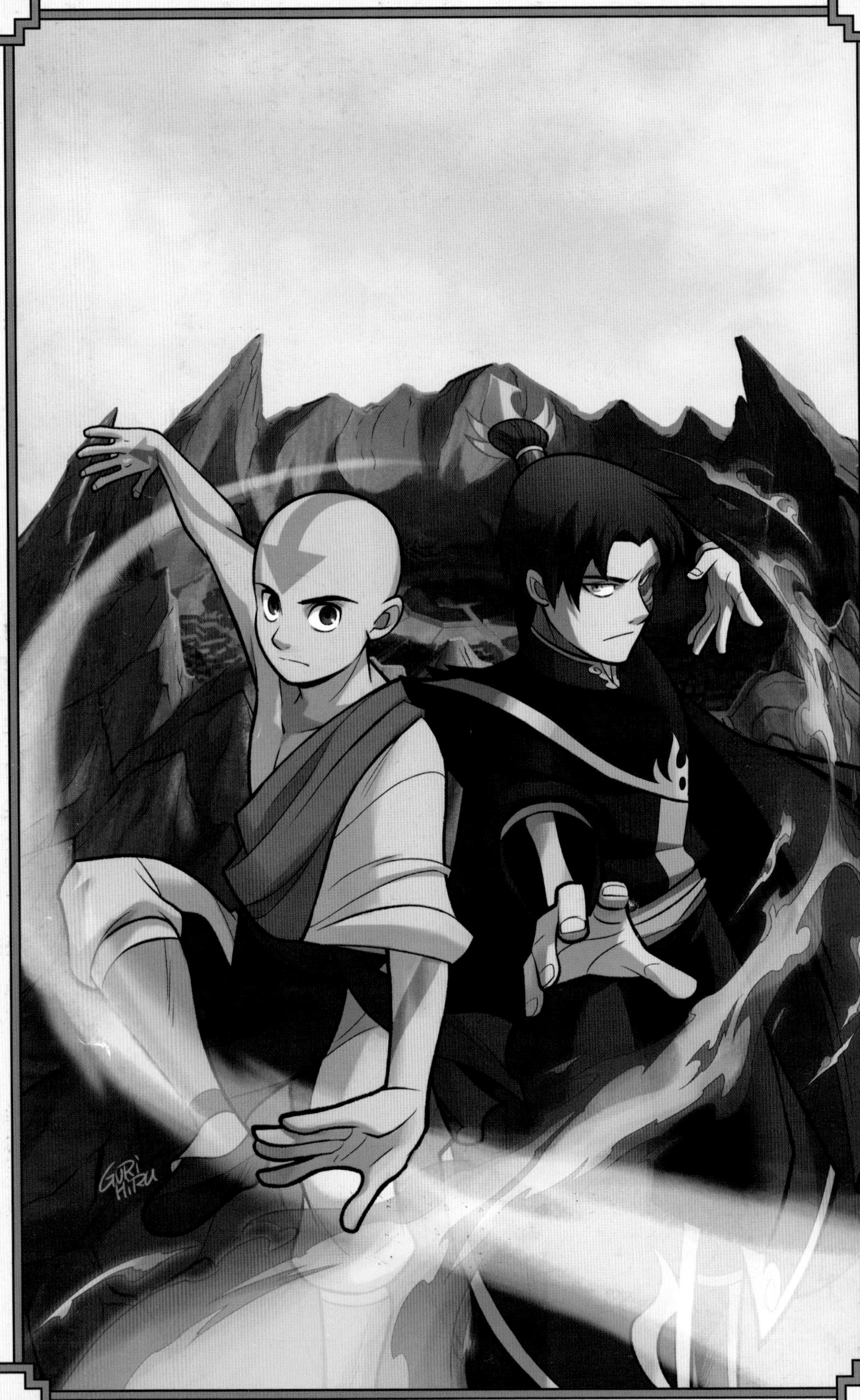
GURI HIRU

nickelodeon

降去神通

AVATAR

THE LAST AIRBENDER

SMOKE AND SHADOW · PART ONE

script
GENE LUEN YANG

art and cover
GURIHIRU

lettering
MICHAEL HEISLER

DARK HORSE BOOKS

president and publisher
MIKE RICHARDSON

editor
DAVE MARSHALL

associate editor
AARON WALKER

collection designer
JUSTIN COUCH

digital art technician
CHRISTINA McKENZIE

Special thanks to Linda Lee, Kat van Dam, James Salerno, and Joan Hilty
at Nickelodeon, and to Bryan Konietzko and Michael Dante DiMartino.

Published by **Dark Horse Books**
A division of Dark Horse Comics LLC
10956 SE Main Street, Milwaukie, OR 97222

DarkHorse.com
Nick.com

International Licensing: (503) 905-2377
To find a comics shop in your area, visit comicshoplocator.com

First edition: September 2015 | ISBN 978-1-61655-761-4

3 5 7 9 10 8 6 4
Printed in China

Neil Hankerson, Executive Vice President • Tom Weddle, Chief Financial Officer • Randy Stradley, Vice President of Publishing • Michael Martens, Vice President of Book Trade Sales • Scott Allie, Editor in Chief • Matt Parkinson, Vice President of Marketing • David Scroggy, Vice President of Product Development • Dale LaFountain, Vice President of Information Technology • Darlene Vogel, Senior Director of Print, Design, and Production • Ken Lizzi, General Counsel • Davey Estrada, Editorial Director • Chris Warner, Senior Books Editor • Cary Grazzini, Director of Print and Development • Lia Ribacchi, Art Director • Cara Niece, Director of Scheduling • Mark Bernardi, Director of Digital Publishing

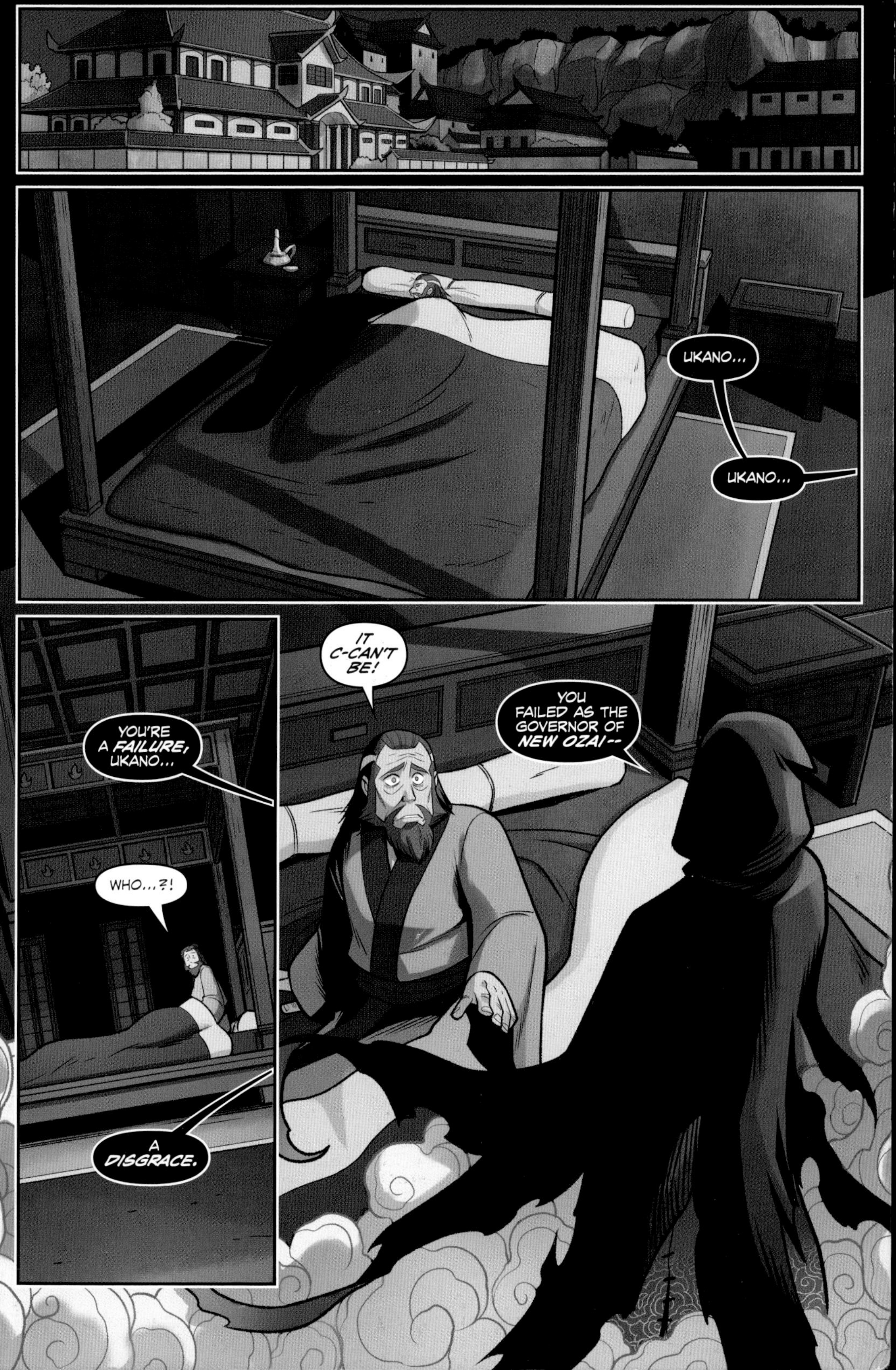
UKANO...
UKANO...
IT C-CAN'T BE!
YOU'RE A FAILURE, UKANO...
WHO...?!
A DISGRACE.
YOU FAILED AS THE GOVERNOR OF NEW OZAI--

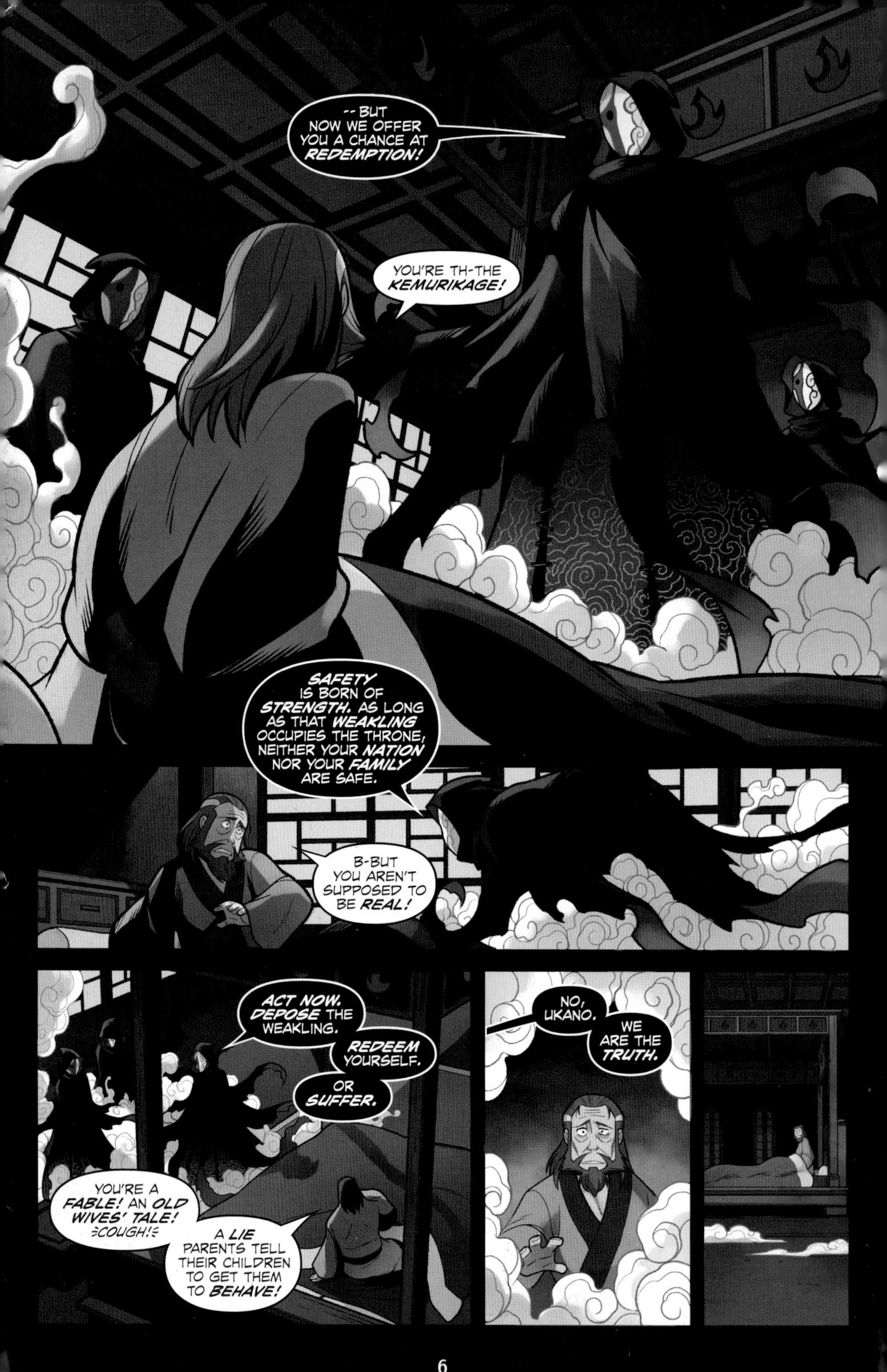
--BUT NOW WE OFFER YOU A CHANCE AT REDEMPTION!
YOU'RE TH-THE KEMURIKAGE!
SAFETY IS BORN OF STRENGTH. AS LONG AS THAT WEAKLING OCCUPIES THE THRONE, NEITHER YOUR NATION NOR YOUR FAMILY ARE SAFE.
B-BUT YOU AREN'T SUPPOSED TO BE REAL!
ACT NOW. DEPOSE THE WEAKLING.
REDEEM YOURSELF.
OR SUFFER.
YOU'RE A FABLE! AN OLD WIVES' TALE! COUGH!
A LIE PARENTS TELL THEIR CHILDREN TO GET THEM TO BEHAVE!
NO, UKANO.
WE ARE THE TRUTH.

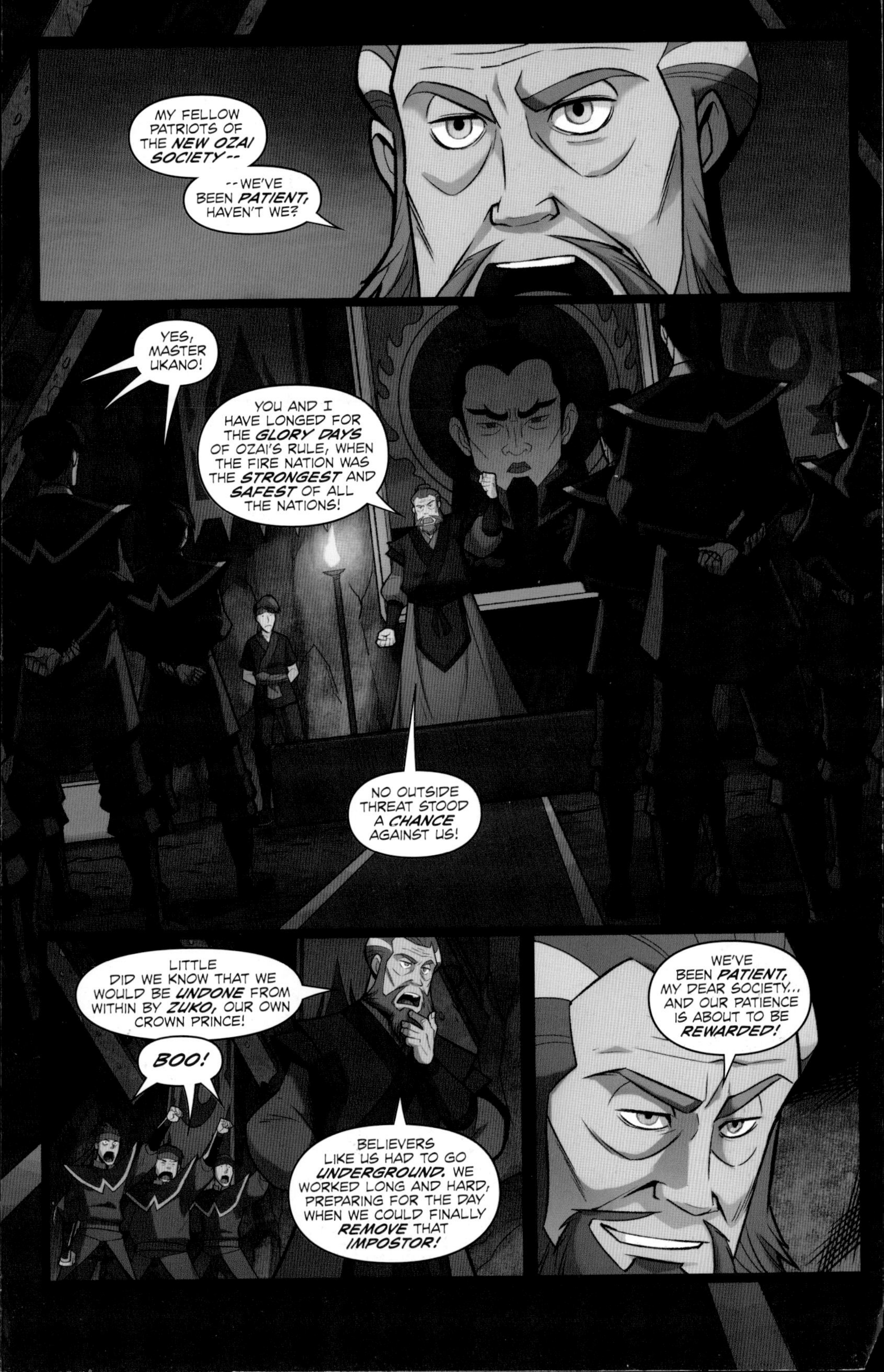
MY FELLOW PATRIOTS OF THE NEW OZAI SOCIETY--
--WE'VE BEEN PATIENT, HAVEN'T WE?
YES, MASTER UKANO!
YOU AND I HAVE LONGED FOR THE GLORY DAYS OF OZAI'S RULE, WHEN THE FIRE NATION WAS THE STRONGEST AND SAFEST OF ALL THE NATIONS!
NO OUTSIDE THREAT STOOD A CHANCE AGAINST US!
LITTLE DID WE KNOW THAT WE WOULD BE UNDONE FROM WITHIN BY ZUKO, OUR OWN CROWN PRINCE!
BOO!
BELIEVERS LIKE US HAD TO GO UNDERGROUND. WE WORKED LONG AND HARD, PREPARING FOR THE DAY WHEN WE COULD FINALLY REMOVE THAT IMPOSTOR!
WE'VE BEEN PATIENT, MY DEAR SOCIETY... AND OUR PATIENCE IS ABOUT TO BE REWARDED!

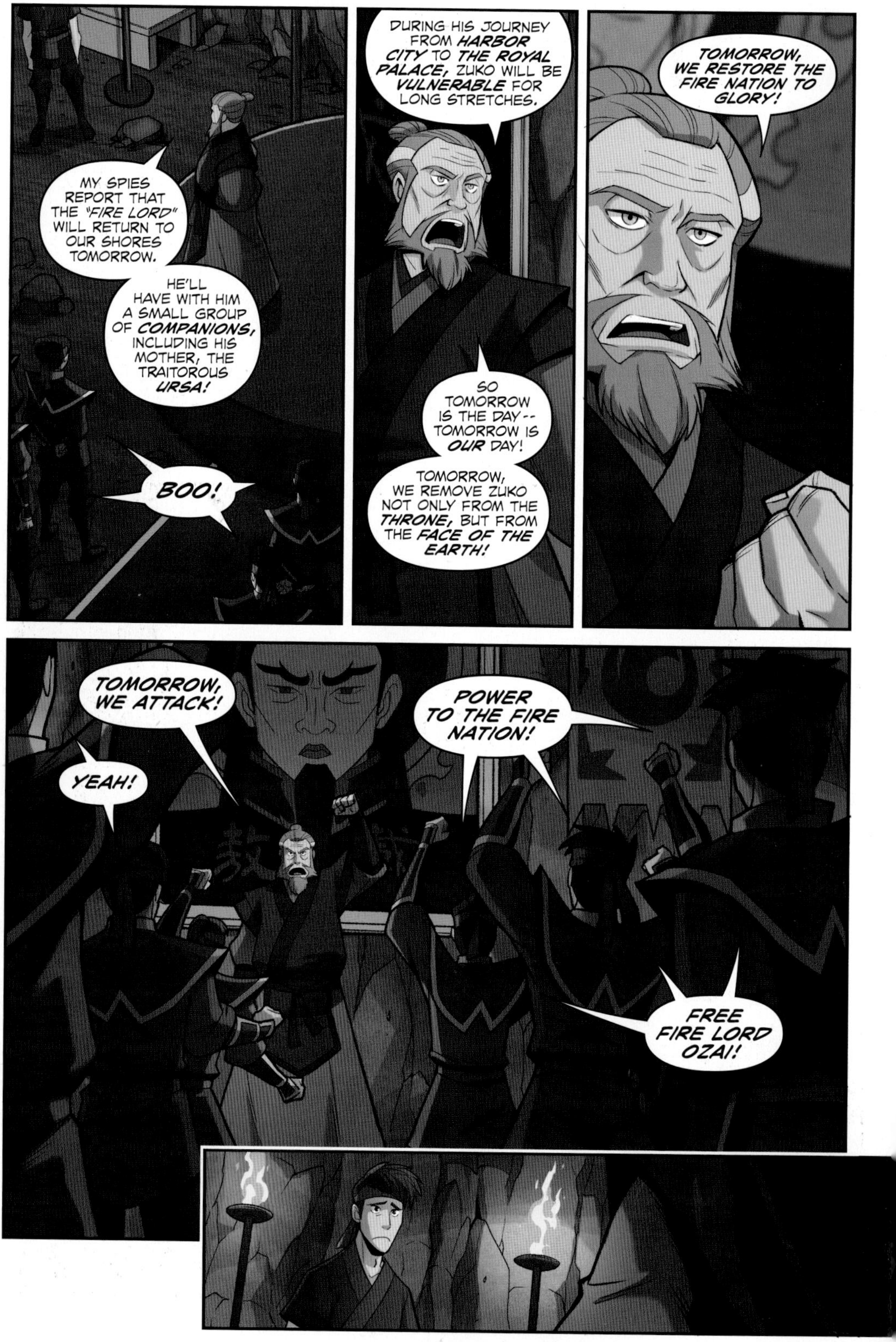
MY SPIES REPORT THAT THE "FIRE LORD" WILL RETURN TO OUR SHORES TOMORROW.
HE'LL HAVE WITH HIM A SMALL GROUP OF COMPANIONS, INCLUDING HIS MOTHER, THE TRAITOROUS URSA!
BOO!
DURING HIS JOURNEY FROM HARBOR CITY TO THE ROYAL PALACE, ZUKO WILL BE VULNERABLE FOR LONG STRETCHES.
SO TOMORROW IS THE DAY-- TOMORROW IS OUR DAY!
TOMORROW, WE REMOVE ZUKO NOT ONLY FROM THE THRONE, BUT FROM THE FACE OF THE EARTH!
TOMORROW, WE RESTORE THE FIRE NATION TO GLORY!
TOMORROW, WE ATTACK!
YEAH!
POWER TO THE FIRE NATION!
FREE FIRE LORD OZAI!

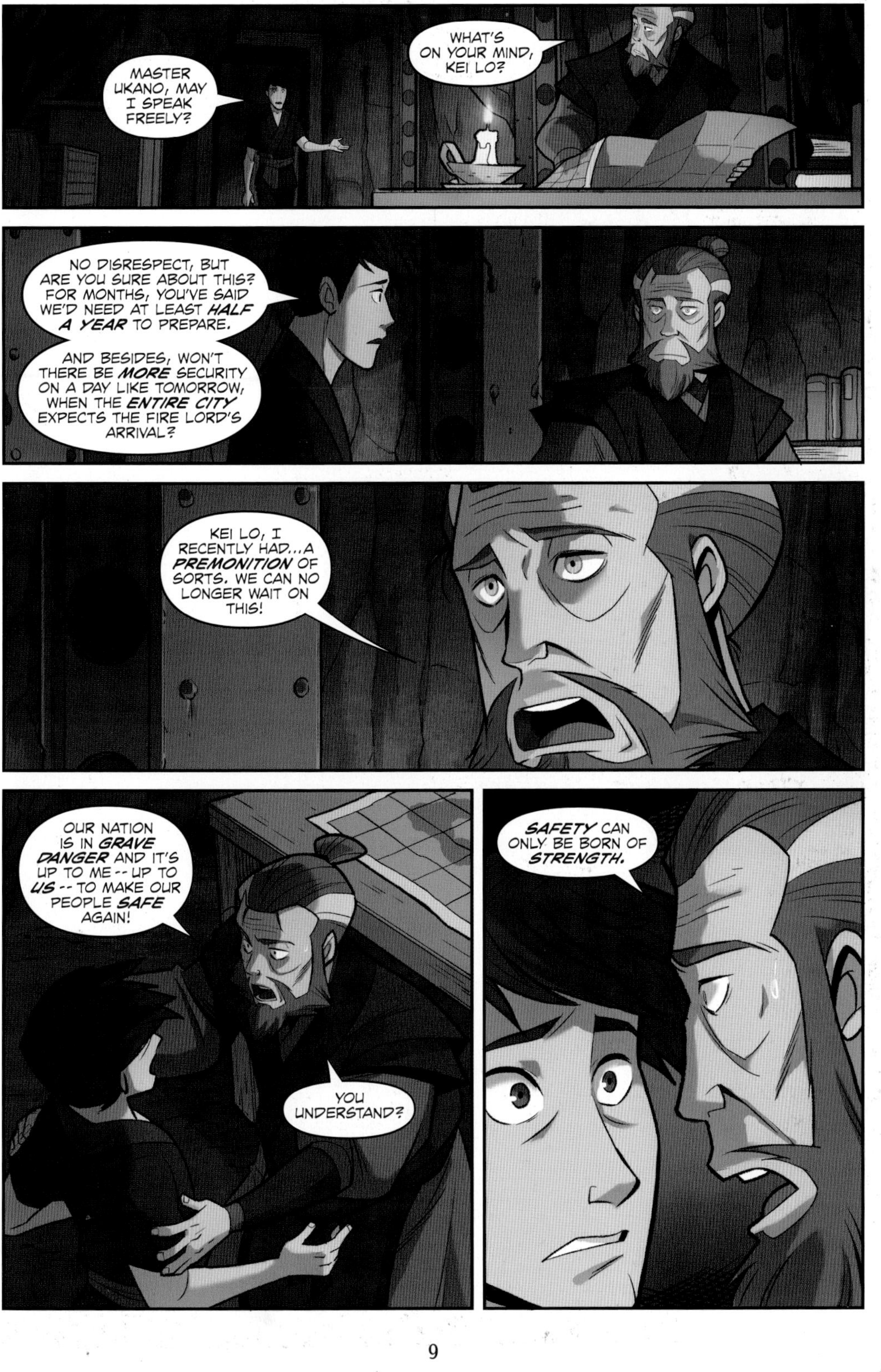
MASTER UKANO, MAY I SPEAK FREELY?
WHAT'S ON YOUR MIND, KEI LO?
NO DISRESPECT, BUT ARE YOU SURE ABOUT THIS? FOR MONTHS, YOU'VE SAID WE'D NEED AT LEAST HALF A YEAR TO PREPARE.
AND BESIDES, WON'T THERE BE MORE SECURITY ON A DAY LIKE TOMORROW, WHEN THE ENTIRE CITY EXPECTS THE FIRE LORD'S ARRIVAL?
KEI LO, I RECENTLY HAD...A PREMONITION OF SORTS. WE CAN NO LONGER WAIT ON THIS!
OUR NATION IS IN GRAVE DANGER AND IT'S UP TO ME -- UP TO US -- TO MAKE OUR PEOPLE SAFE AGAIN!
YOU UNDERSTAND?
SAFETY CAN ONLY BE BORN OF STRENGTH.

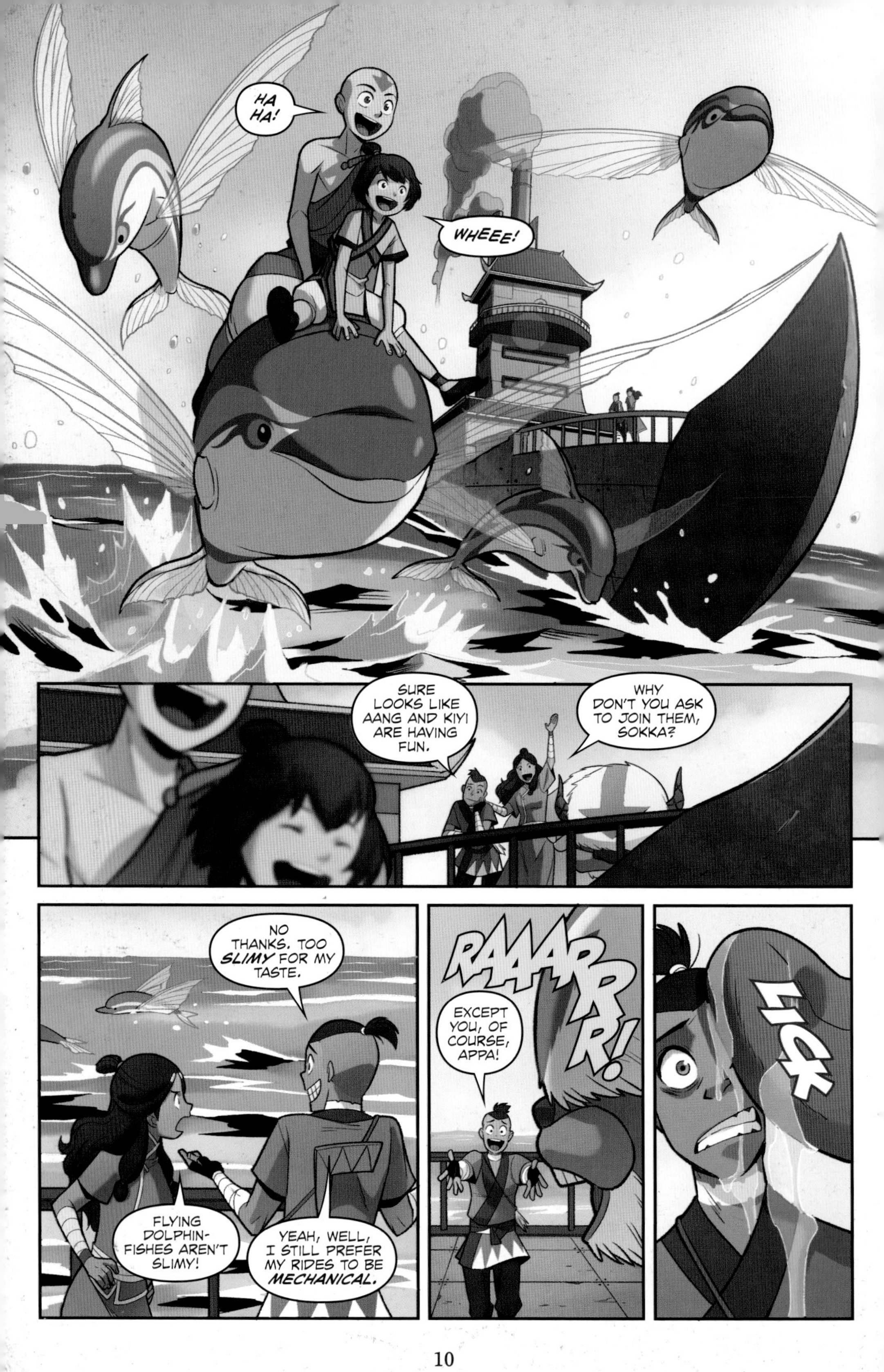
HA HA!
WHEEE!
SURE LOOKS LIKE AANG AND KIYI ARE HAVING FUN.
WHY DON'T YOU ASK TO JOIN THEM, SOKKA?
NO THANKS. TOO SLIMY FOR MY TASTE.
FLYING DOLPHIN-FISHES AREN'T SLIMY!
YEAH, WELL, I STILL PREFER MY RIDES TO BE MECHANICAL.
RAAARRR!
EXCEPT YOU, OF COURSE, APPA!
LICK

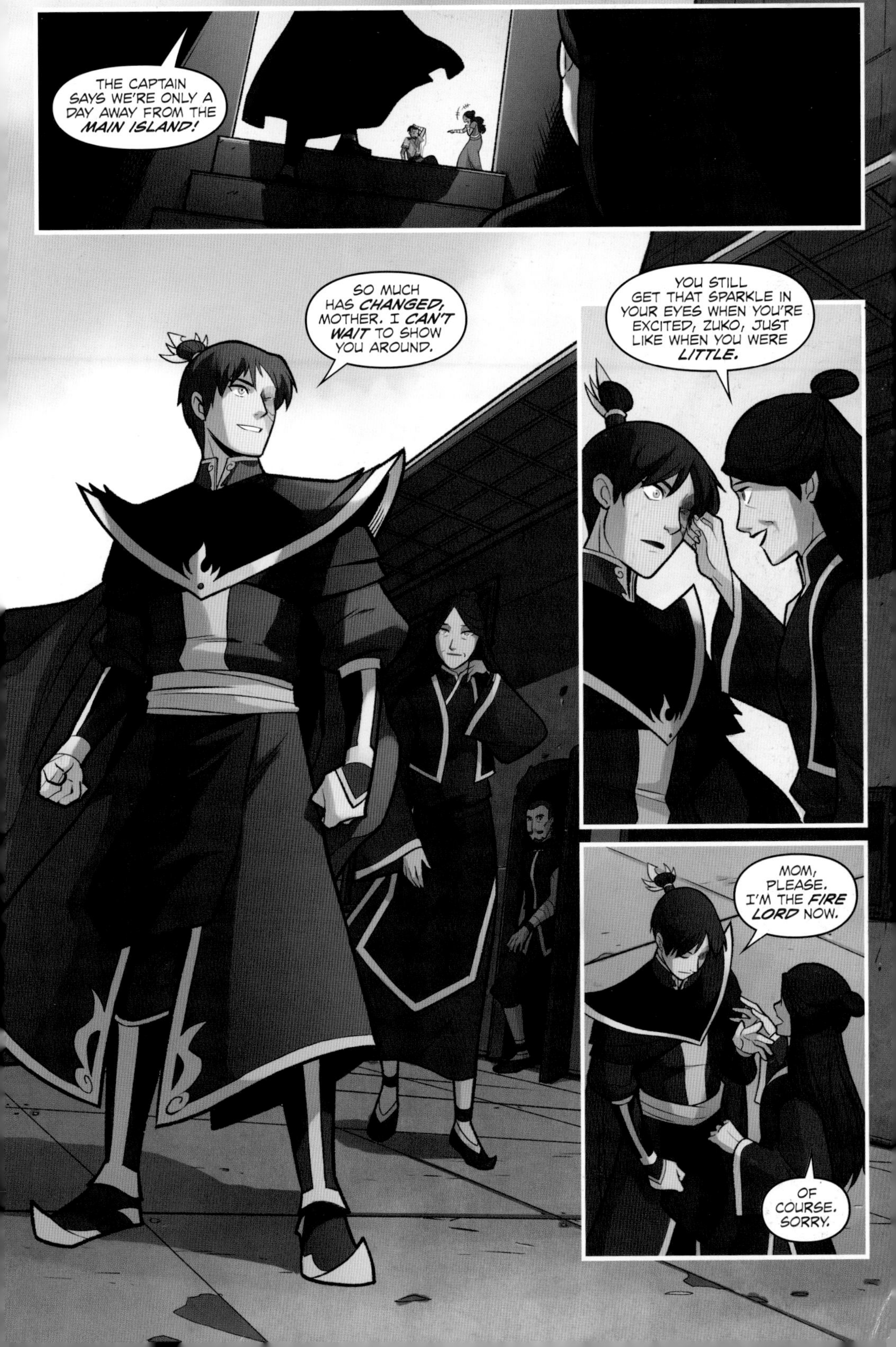

THE CAPTAIN SAYS WE'RE ONLY A DAY AWAY FROM THE MAIN ISLAND!
SO MUCH HAS CHANGED, MOTHER. I CAN'T WAIT TO SHOW YOU AROUND.
YOU STILL GET THAT SPARKLE IN YOUR EYES WHEN YOU'RE EXCITED, ZUKO, JUST LIKE WHEN YOU WERE LITTLE.
MOM, PLEASE. I'M THE FIRE LORD NOW.
OF COURSE. SORRY.

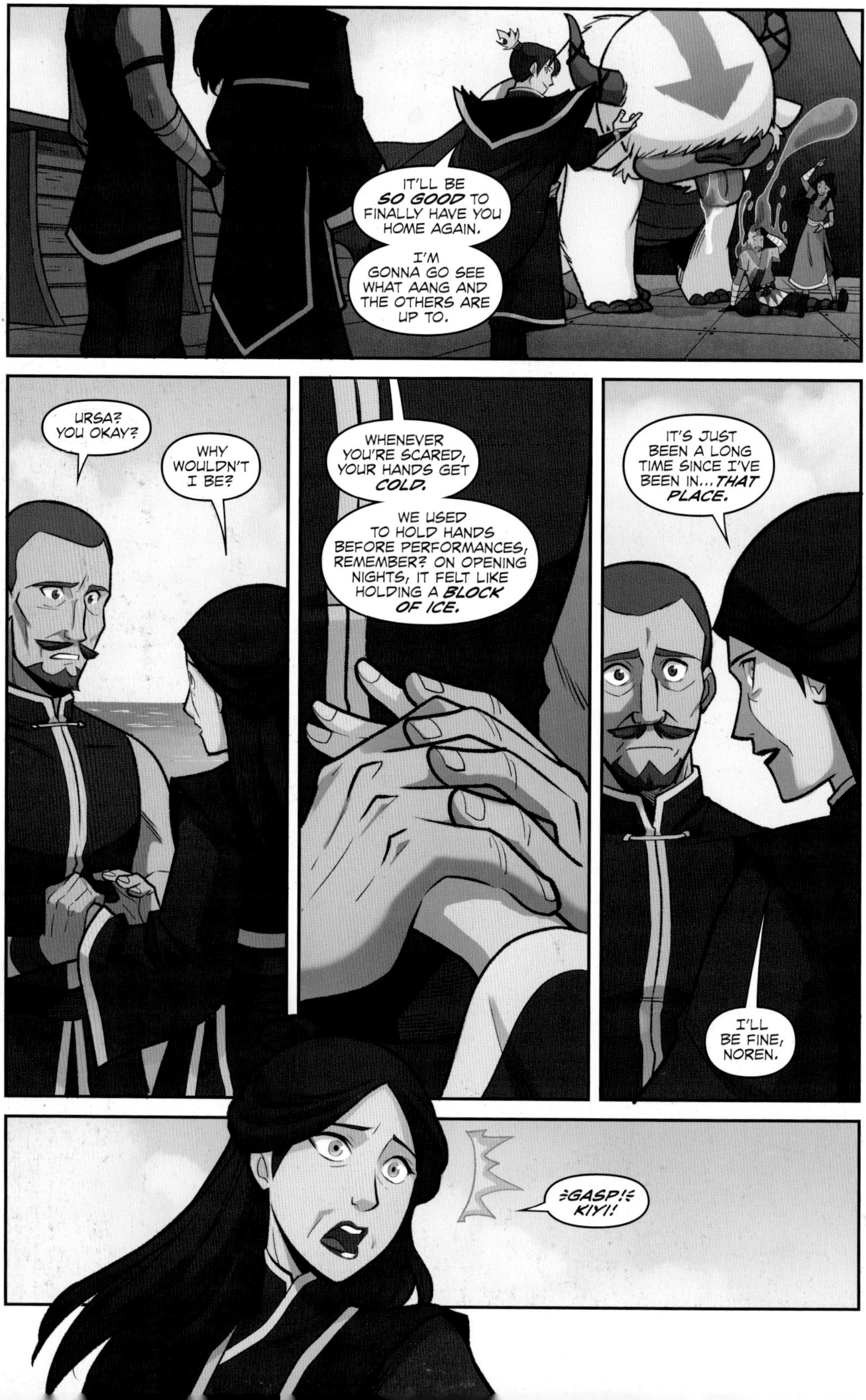
IT'LL BE SO GOOD TO FINALLY HAVE YOU HOME AGAIN.
I'M GONNA GO SEE WHAT AANG AND THE OTHERS ARE UP TO.
URSA? YOU OKAY?
WHY WOULDN'T I BE?
WHENEVER YOU'RE SCARED, YOUR HANDS GET COLD.
WE USED TO HOLD HANDS BEFORE PERFORMANCES, REMEMBER? ON OPENING NIGHTS, IT FELT LIKE HOLDING A BLOCK OF ICE.
IT'S JUST BEEN A LONG TIME SINCE I'VE BEEN IN... THAT PLACE.
I'LL BE FINE, NOREN.
GASP! KIYI!

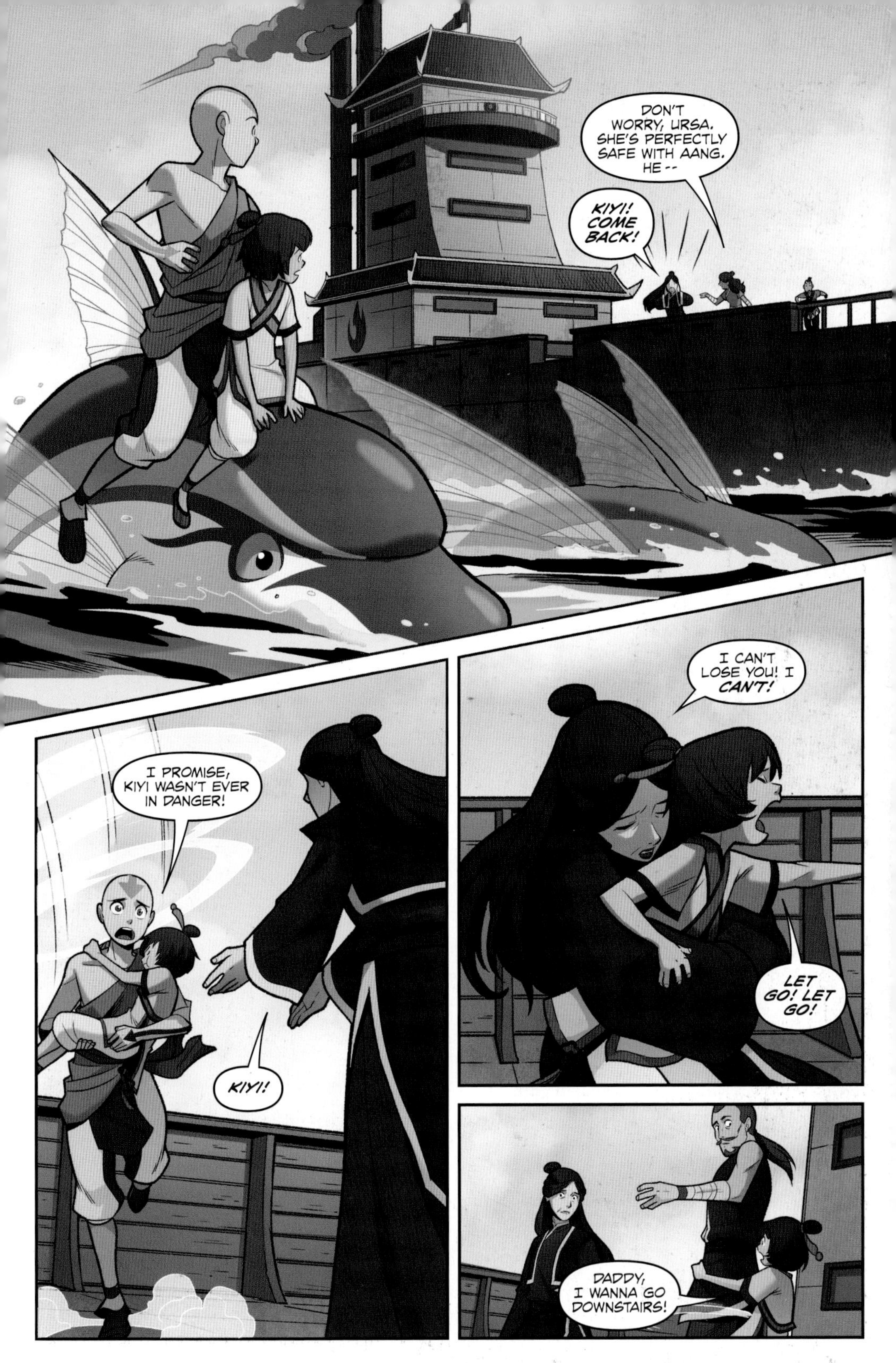

DON'T WORRY, URSA. SHE'S PERFECTLY SAFE WITH AANG. HE --
KIYI! COME BACK!
I PROMISE, KIYI WASN'T EVER IN DANGER!
KIYI!
I CAN'T LOSE YOU! I CAN'T!
LET GO! LET GO!
DADDY, I WANNA GO DOWNSTAIRS!

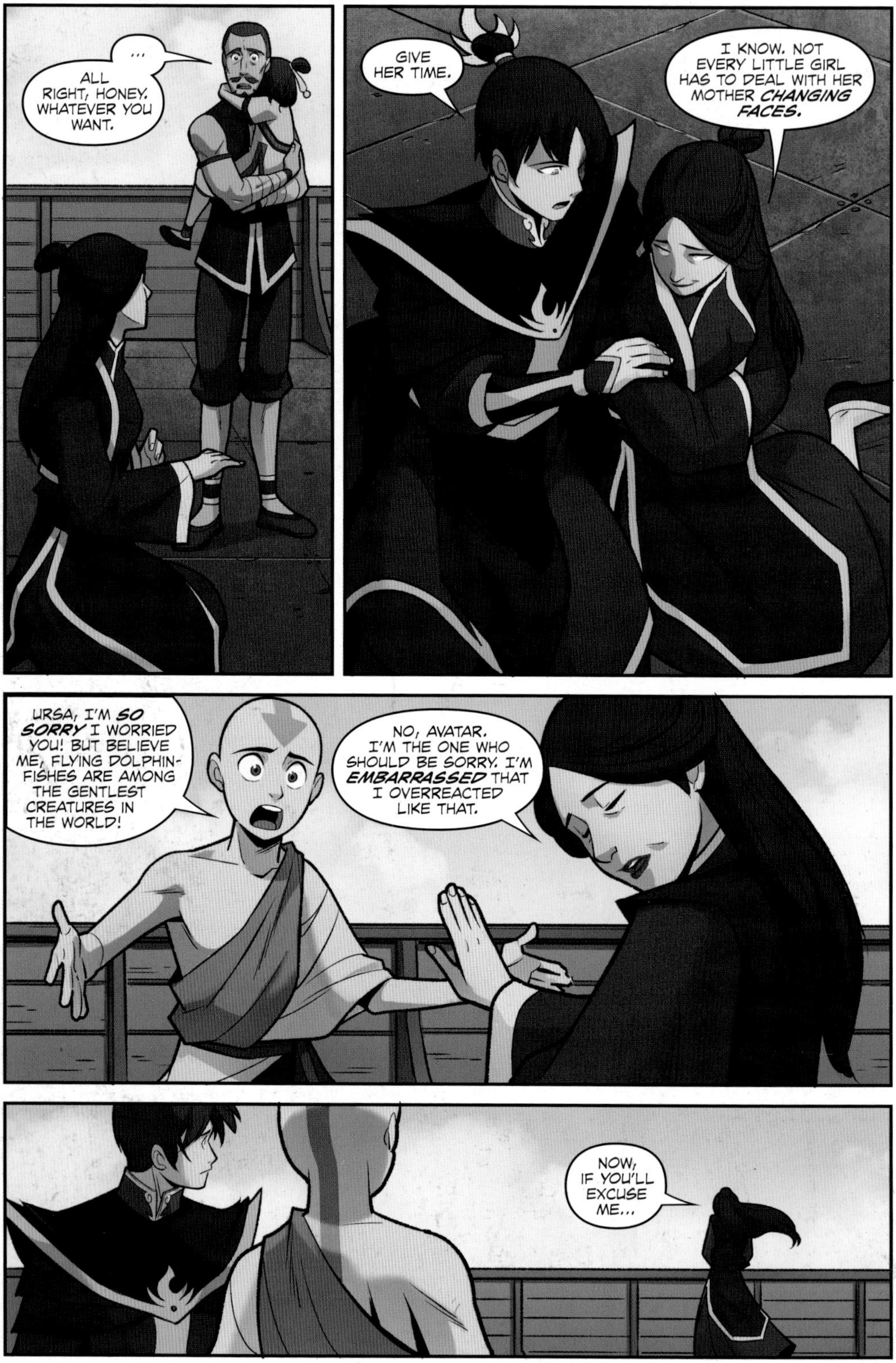
...
ALL RIGHT, HONEY. WHATEVER YOU WANT.
GIVE HER TIME.
I KNOW. NOT EVERY LITTLE GIRL HAS TO DEAL WITH HER MOTHER CHANGING FACES.
URSA, I'M SO SORRY I WORRIED YOU! BUT BELIEVE ME, FLYING DOLPHIN-FISHES ARE AMONG THE GENTLEST CREATURES IN THE WORLD!
NO, AVATAR. I'M THE ONE WHO SHOULD BE SORRY. I'M EMBARRASSED THAT I OVERREACTED LIKE THAT.
NOW, IF YOU'LL EXCUSE ME...

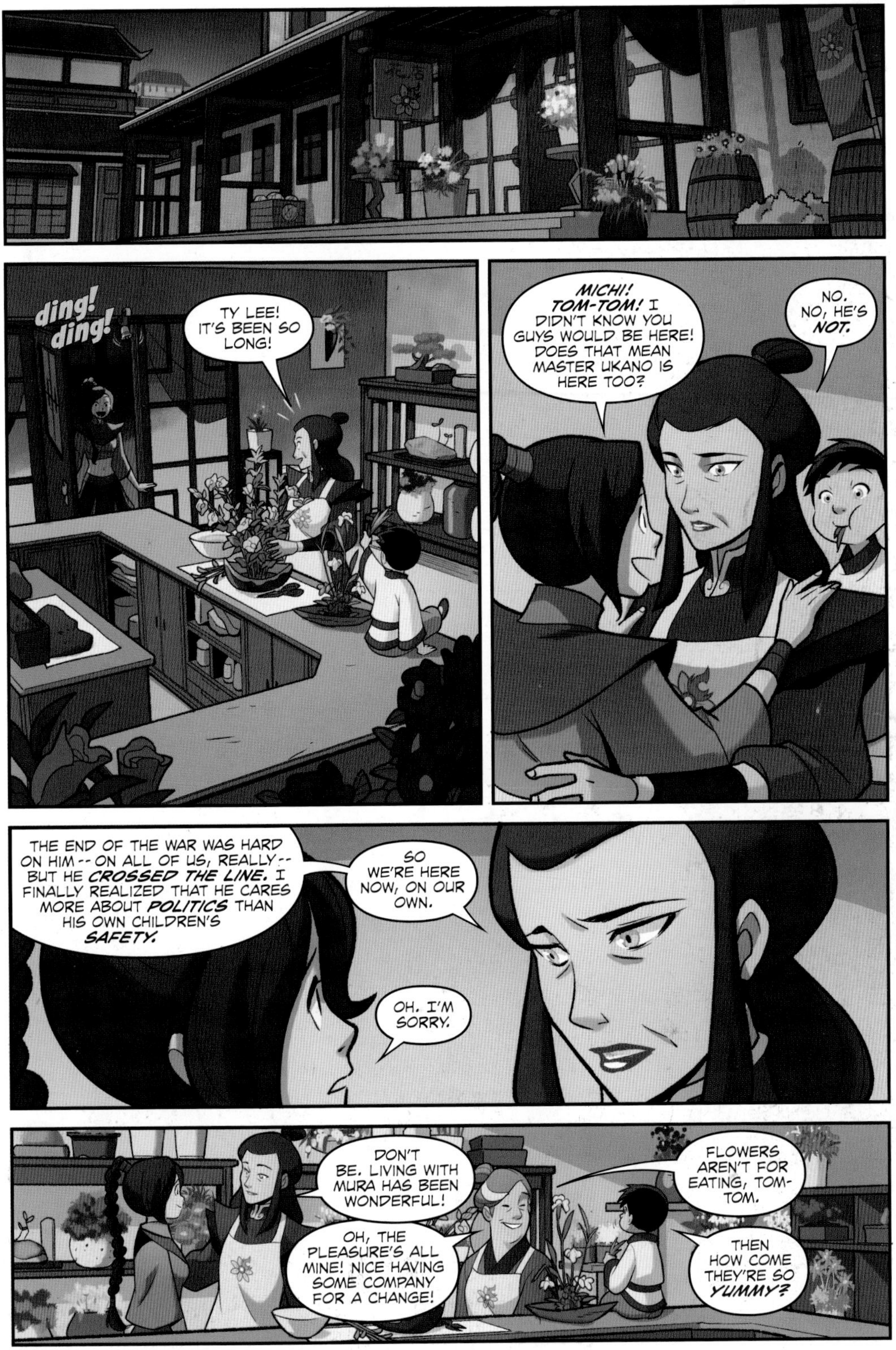
ding! ding!
TY LEE! IT'S BEEN SO LONG!
MICHI! TOM-TOM! I DIDN'T KNOW YOU GUYS WOULD BE HERE! DOES THAT MEAN MASTER UKANO IS HERE TOO?
NO. NO, HE'S NOT.
THE END OF THE WAR WAS HARD ON HIM--ON ALL OF US, REALLY--BUT HE CROSSED THE LINE. I FINALLY REALIZED THAT HE CARES MORE ABOUT POLITICS THAN HIS OWN CHILDREN'S SAFETY.
SO WE'RE HERE NOW, ON OUR OWN.
OH. I'M SORRY.
DON'T BE. LIVING WITH MURA HAS BEEN WONDERFUL!
OH, THE PLEASURE'S ALL MINE! NICE HAVING SOME COMPANY FOR A CHANGE!
FLOWERS AREN'T FOR EATING, TOM-TOM.
THEN HOW COME THEY'RE SO YUMMY?

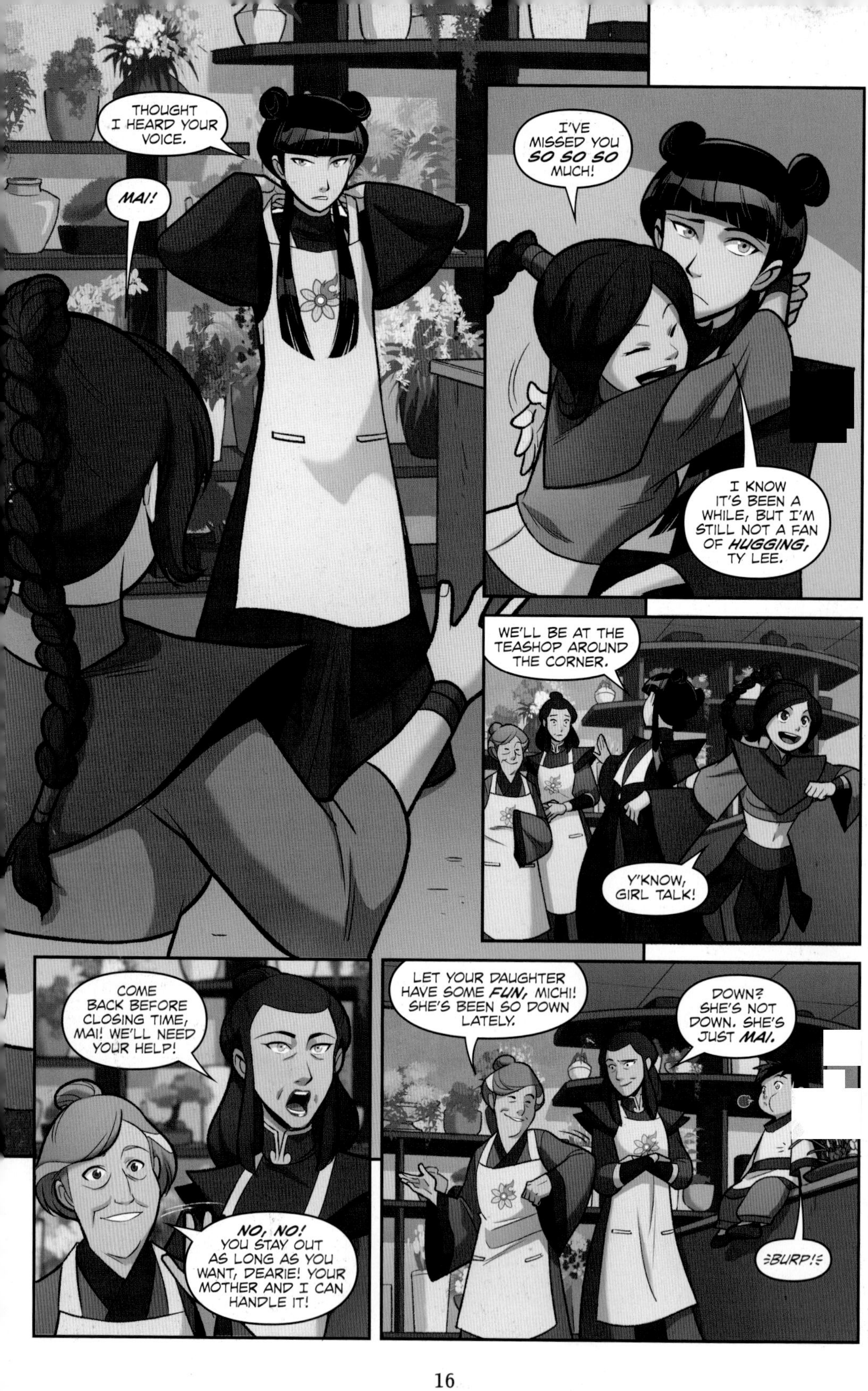
THOUGHT I HEARD YOUR VOICE.
MAI!
I'VE MISSED YOU SO SO SO MUCH!
I KNOW IT'S BEEN A WHILE, BUT I'M STILL NOT A FAN OF HUGGING, TY LEE.
WE'LL BE AT THE TEASHOP AROUND THE CORNER.
Y'KNOW, GIRL TALK!
COME BACK BEFORE CLOSING TIME, MAI! WE'LL NEED YOUR HELP!
NO, NO! YOU STAY OUT AS LONG AS YOU WANT, DEARIE! YOUR MOTHER AND I CAN HANDLE IT!
LET YOUR DAUGHTER HAVE SOME FUN, MICHI! SHE'S BEEN SO DOWN LATELY.
DOWN? SHE'S NOT DOWN. SHE'S JUST MAI.
BURP!

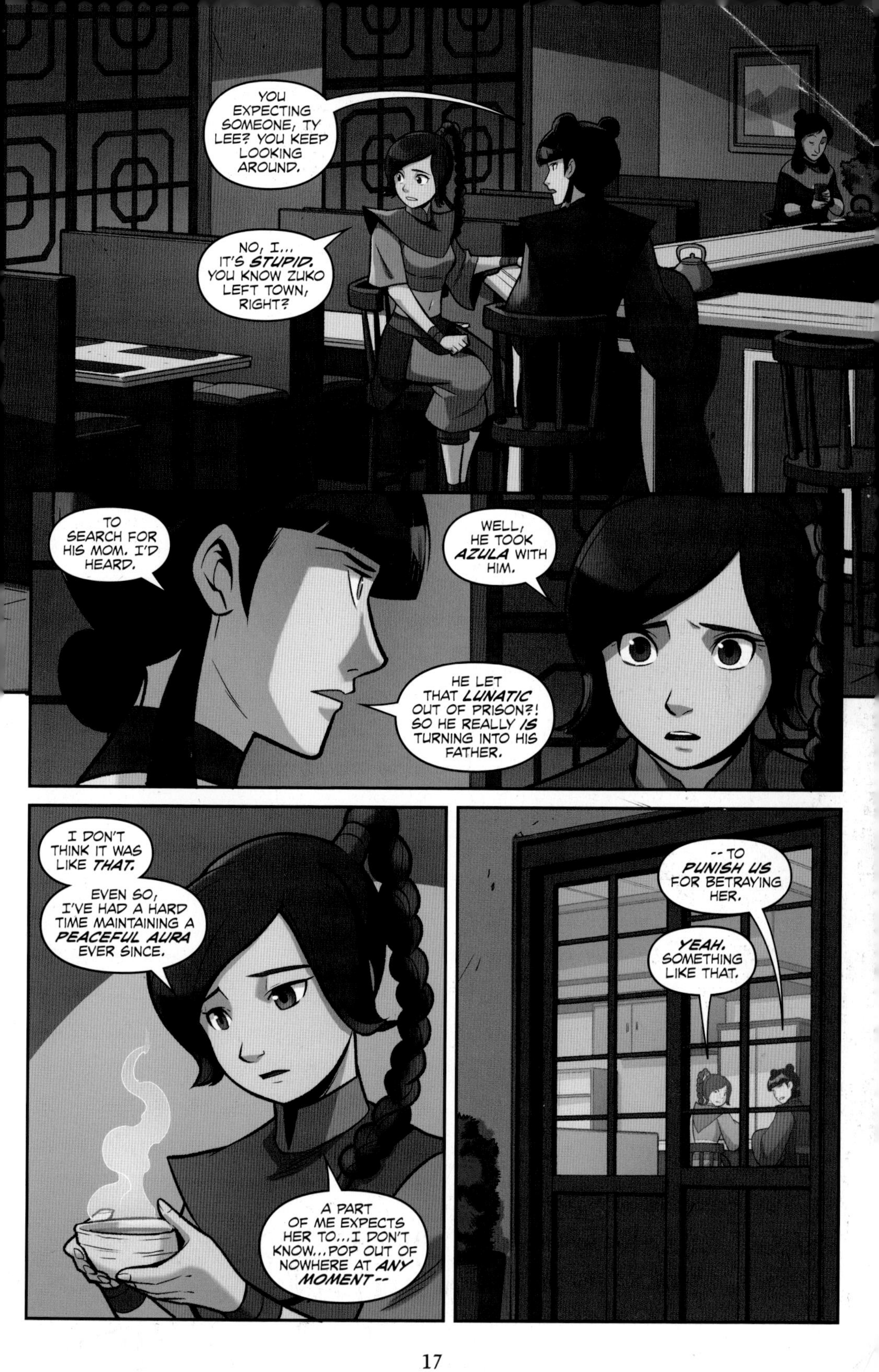

YOU EXPECTING SOMEONE, TY LEE? YOU KEEP LOOKING AROUND.
NO, I... IT'S STUPID. YOU KNOW ZUKO LEFT TOWN, RIGHT?
TO SEARCH FOR HIS MOM. I'D HEARD.
WELL, HE TOOK AZULA WITH HIM.
HE LET THAT LUNATIC OUT OF PRISON?! SO HE REALLY IS TURNING INTO HIS FATHER.
I DON'T THINK IT WAS LIKE THAT.
EVEN SO, I'VE HAD A HARD TIME MAINTAINING A PEACEFUL AURA EVER SINCE.
A PART OF ME EXPECTS HER TO...I DON'T KNOW...POP OUT OF NOWHERE AT ANY MOMENT--
--TO PUNISH US FOR BETRAYING HER.
YEAH. SOMETHING LIKE THAT.

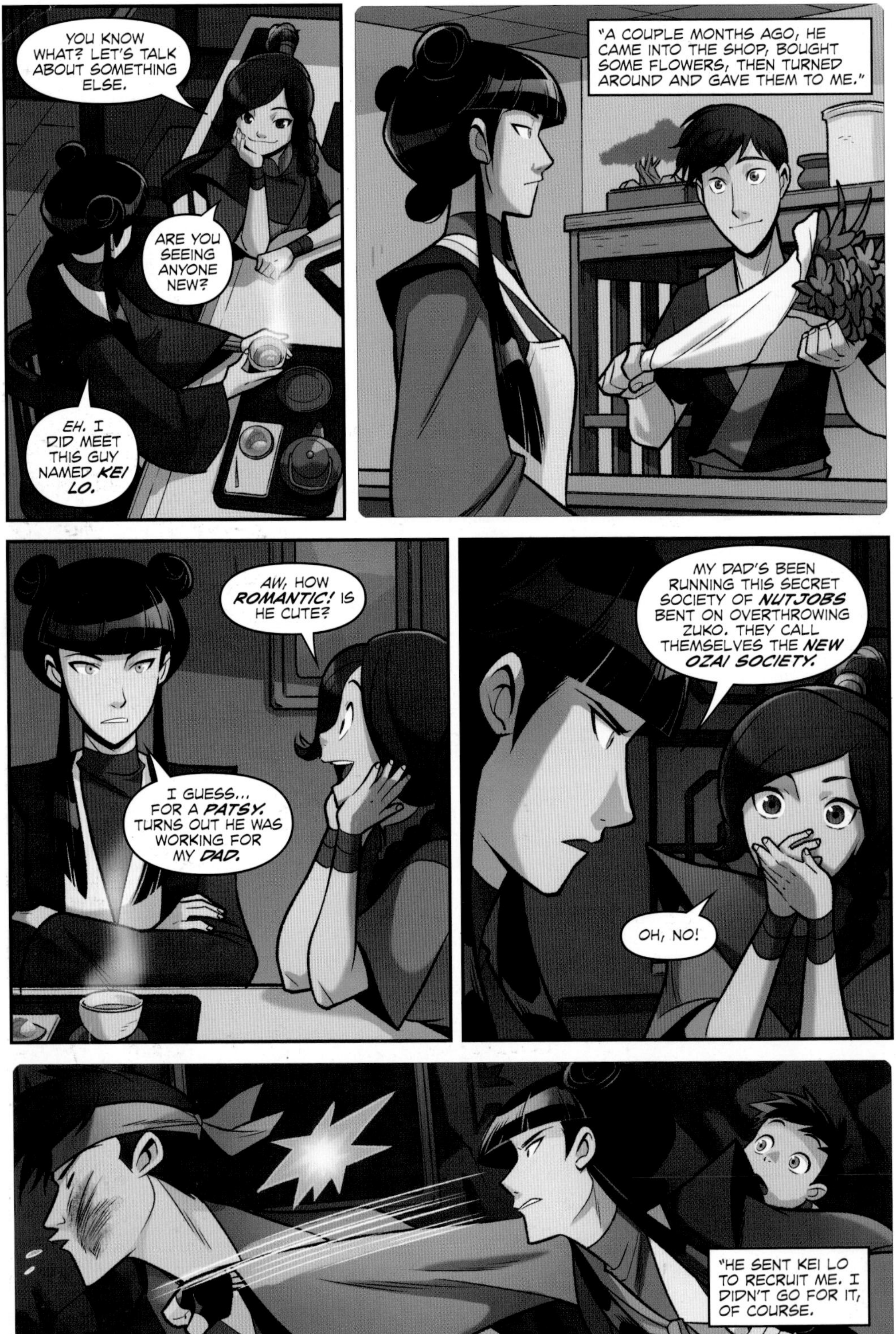
YOU KNOW WHAT? LET'S TALK ABOUT SOMETHING ELSE.
ARE YOU SEEING ANYONE NEW?
EH. I DID MEET THIS GUY NAMED KEI LO.
"A COUPLE MONTHS AGO, HE CAME INTO THE SHOP, BOUGHT SOME FLOWERS, THEN TURNED AROUND AND GAVE THEM TO ME."
AW, HOW ROMANTIC! IS HE CUTE?
I GUESS... FOR A PATSY. TURNS OUT HE WAS WORKING FOR MY DAD.
MY DAD'S BEEN RUNNING THIS SECRET SOCIETY OF NUTJOBS BENT ON OVERTHROWING ZUKO. THEY CALL THEMSELVES THE NEW OZAI SOCIETY.
OH, NO!
"HE SENT KEI LO TO RECRUIT ME. I DIDN'T GO FOR IT, OF COURSE.

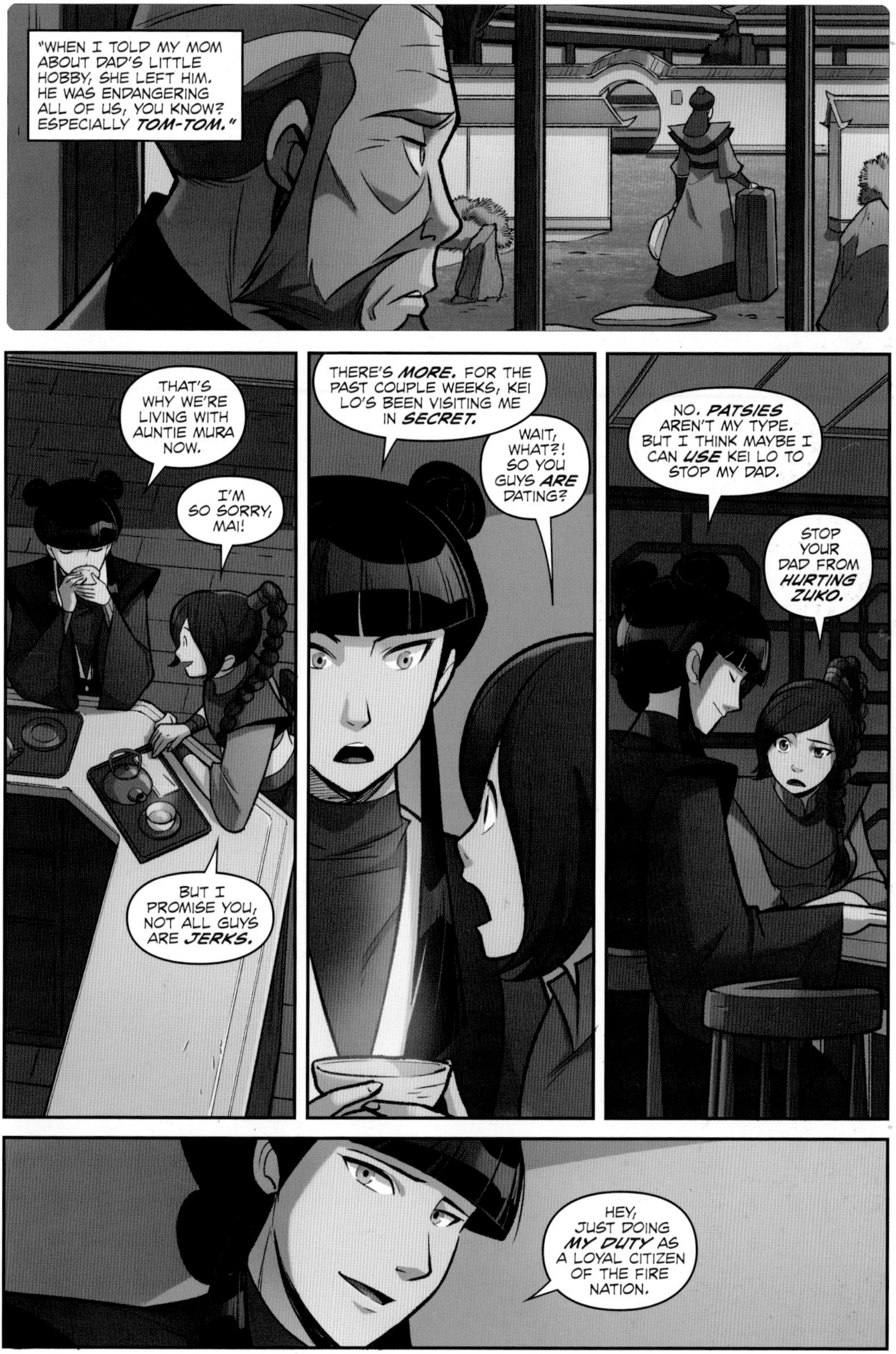
"WHEN I TOLD MY MOM ABOUT DAD'S LITTLE HOBBY, SHE LEFT HIM. HE WAS ENDANGERING ALL OF US, YOU KNOW? ESPECIALLY TOM-TOM."
THAT'S WHY WE'RE LIVING WITH AUNTIE MURA NOW.
I'M SO SORRY, MAI!
BUT I PROMISE YOU, NOT ALL GUYS ARE JERKS.
THERE'S MORE. FOR THE PAST COUPLE WEEKS, KEI LO'S BEEN VISITING ME IN SECRET.
WAIT, WHAT?! SO YOU GUYS ARE DATING?
NO. PATSIES AREN'T MY TYPE. BUT I THINK MAYBE I CAN USE KEI LO TO STOP MY DAD.
STOP YOUR DAD FROM HURTING ZUKO.
HEY, JUST DOING MY DUTY AS A LOYAL CITIZEN OF THE FIRE NATION.

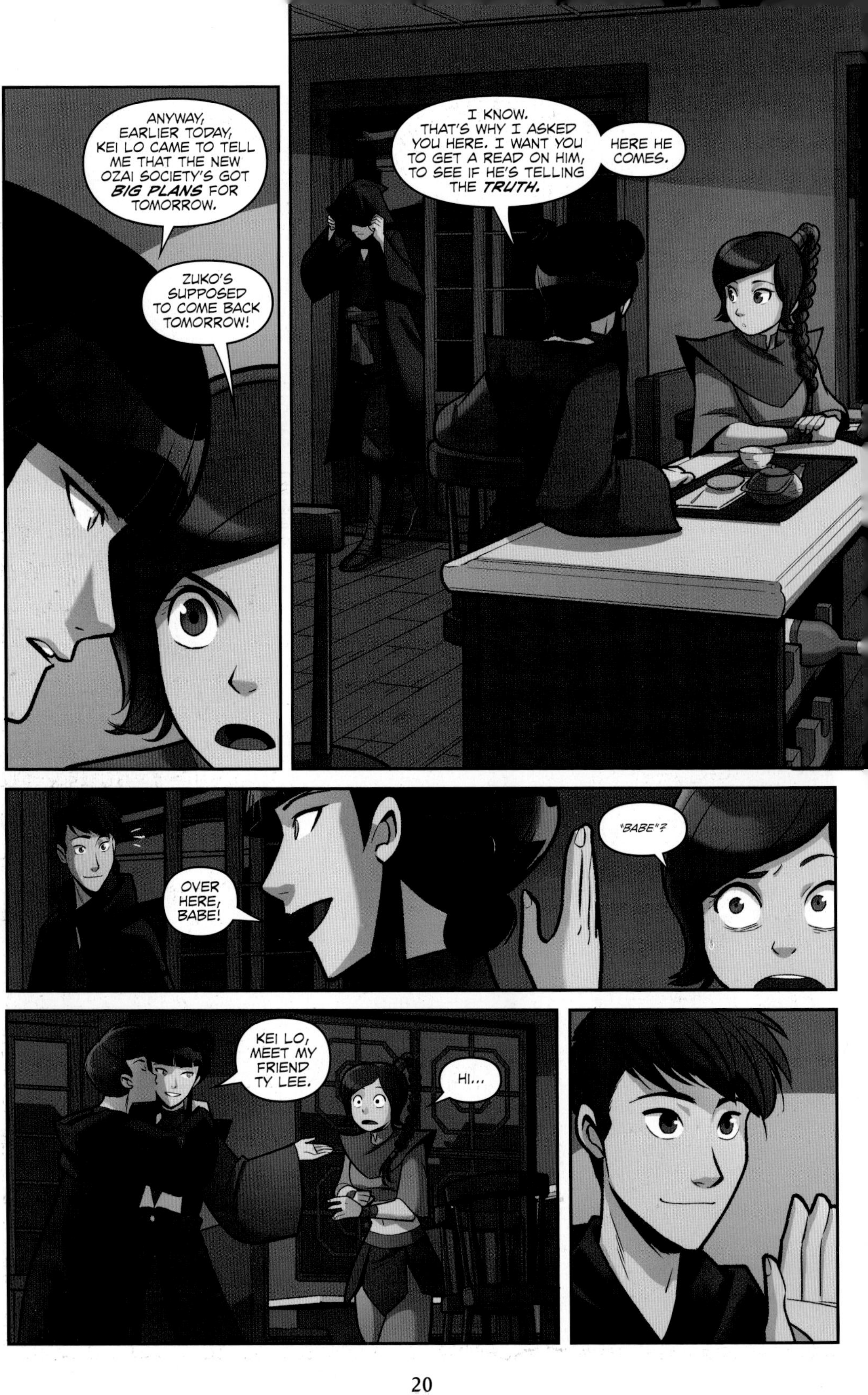
ANYWAY, EARLIER TODAY, KEI LO CAME TO TELL ME THAT THE NEW OZAI SOCIETY'S GOT BIG PLANS FOR TOMORROW.
ZUKO'S SUPPOSED TO COME BACK TOMORROW!
I KNOW. THAT'S WHY I ASKED YOU HERE. I WANT YOU TO GET A READ ON HIM, TO SEE IF HE'S TELLING THE TRUTH.
HERE HE COMES.
OVER HERE, BABE!
"BABE"?
KEI LO, MEET MY FRIEND TY LEE.
HI...

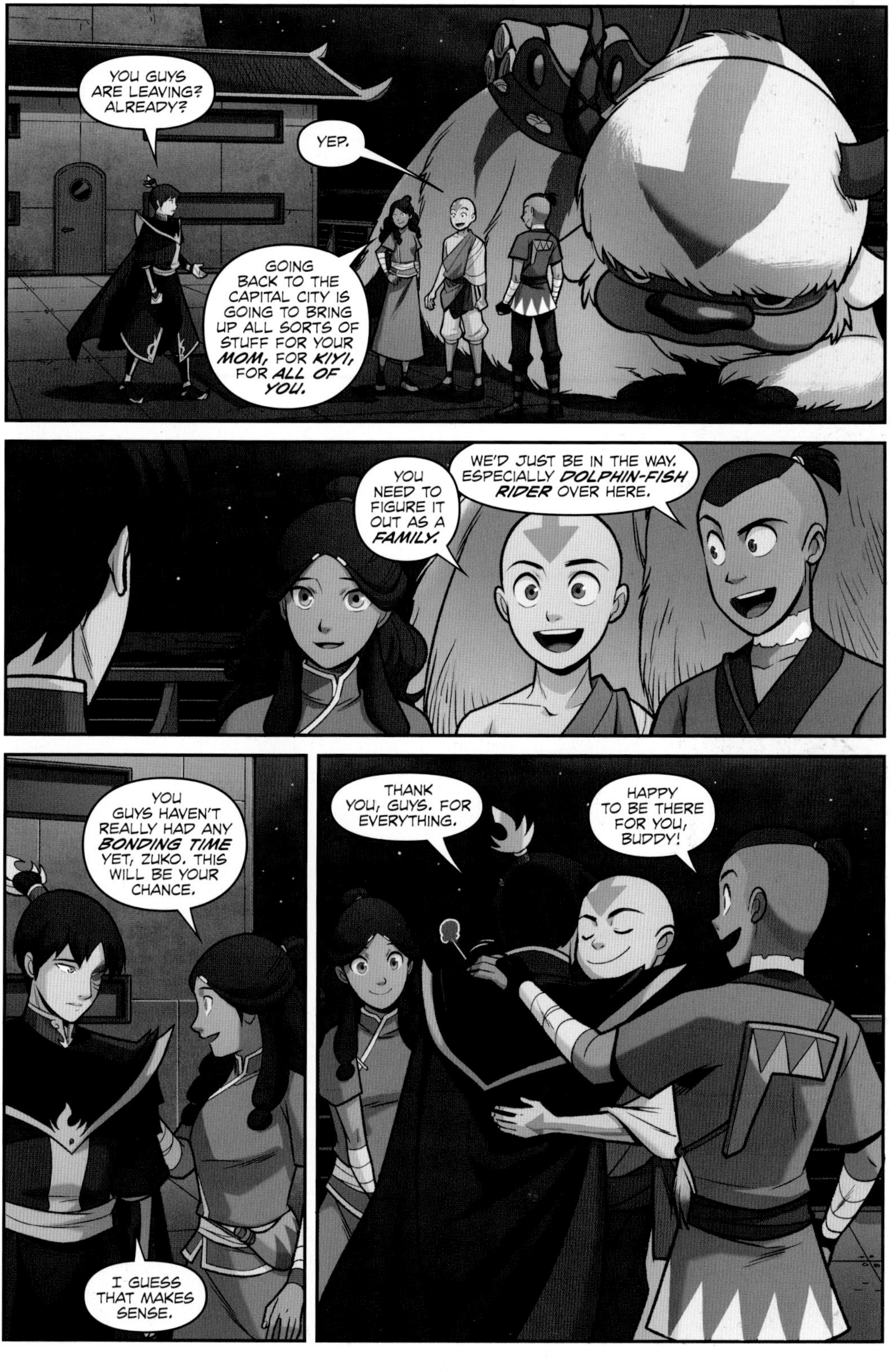
YOU GUYS ARE LEAVING? ALREADY?
YEP.
GOING BACK TO THE CAPITAL CITY IS GOING TO BRING UP ALL SORTS OF STUFF FOR YOUR ***MOM,*** FOR ***KIYI,*** FOR ***ALL OF YOU.***
YOU NEED TO FIGURE IT OUT AS A ***FAMILY.***
WE'D JUST BE IN THE WAY. ESPECIALLY ***DOLPHIN-FISH RIDER*** OVER HERE.
YOU GUYS HAVEN'T REALLY HAD ANY ***BONDING TIME*** YET, ZUKO. THIS WILL BE YOUR CHANCE.
I GUESS THAT MAKES SENSE.
THANK YOU, GUYS. FOR EVERYTHING.
HAPPY TO BE THERE FOR YOU, BUDDY!

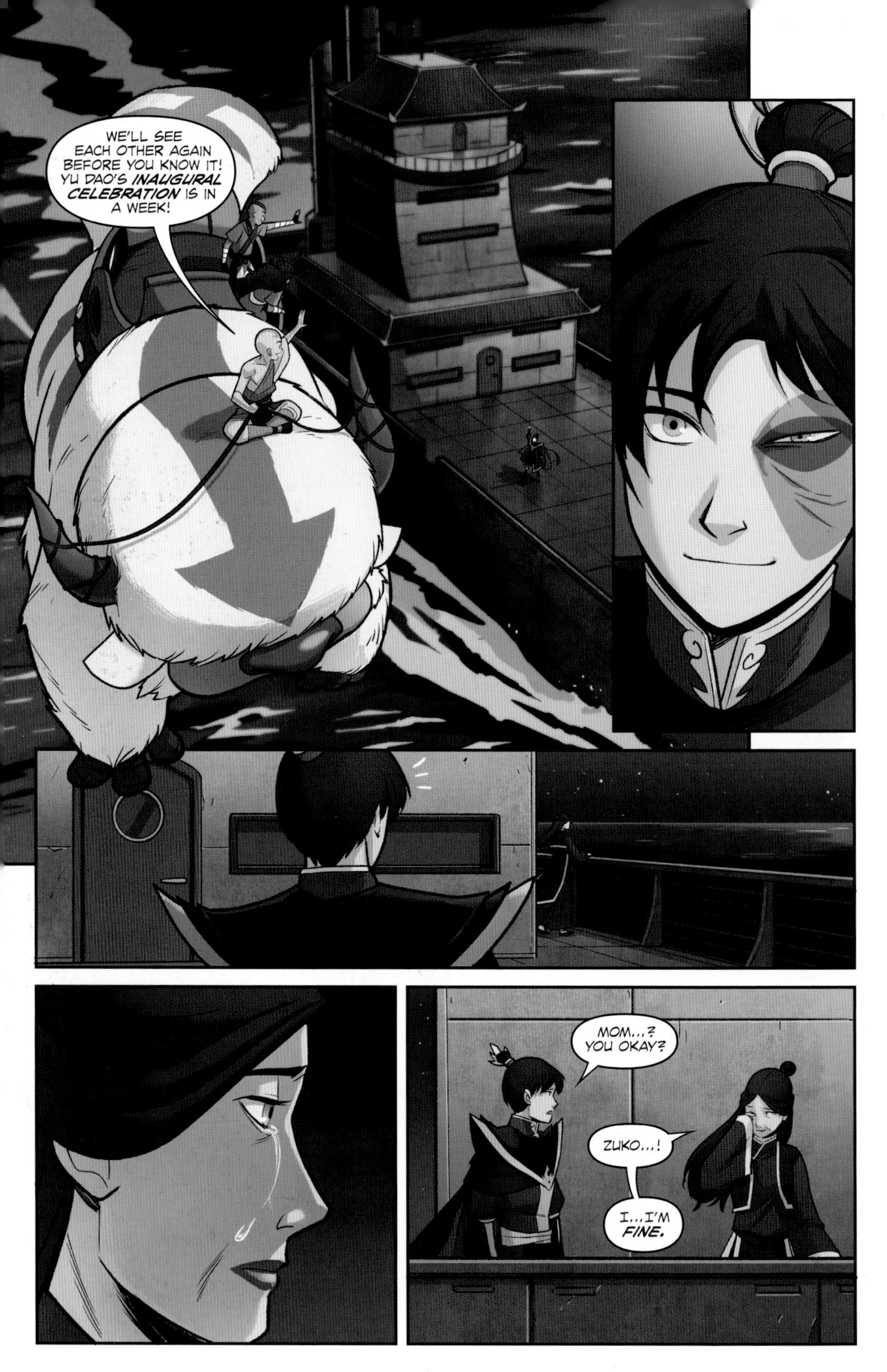
WE'LL SEE EACH OTHER AGAIN BEFORE YOU KNOW IT! YU DAO'S INAUGURAL CELEBRATION IS IN A WEEK!
MOM...? YOU OKAY?
ZUKO...!
I...I'M FINE.

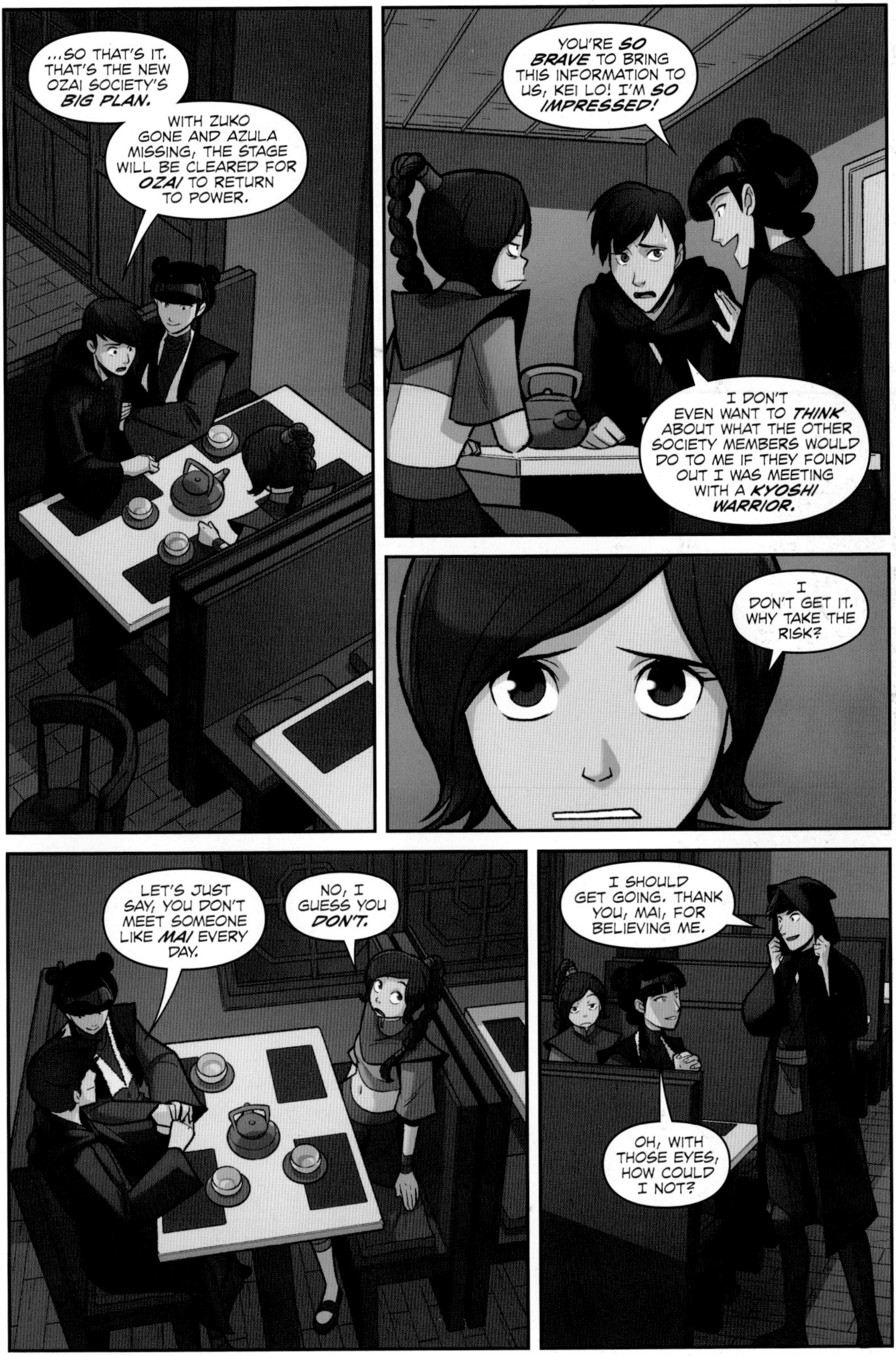
...SO THAT'S IT. THAT'S THE NEW OZAI SOCIETY'S BIG PLAN.
WITH ZUKO GONE AND AZULA MISSING, THE STAGE WILL BE CLEARED FOR OZAI TO RETURN TO POWER.
YOU'RE SO BRAVE TO BRING THIS INFORMATION TO US, KEI LO! I'M SO IMPRESSED!
I DON'T EVEN WANT TO THINK ABOUT WHAT THE OTHER SOCIETY MEMBERS WOULD DO TO ME IF THEY FOUND OUT I WAS MEETING WITH A KYOSHI WARRIOR.
I DON'T GET IT. WHY TAKE THE RISK?
LET'S JUST SAY, YOU DON'T MEET SOMEONE LIKE MAI EVERY DAY.
NO, I GUESS YOU DON'T.
I SHOULD GET GOING. THANK YOU, MAI, FOR BELIEVING ME.
OH, WITH THOSE EYES, HOW COULD I NOT?

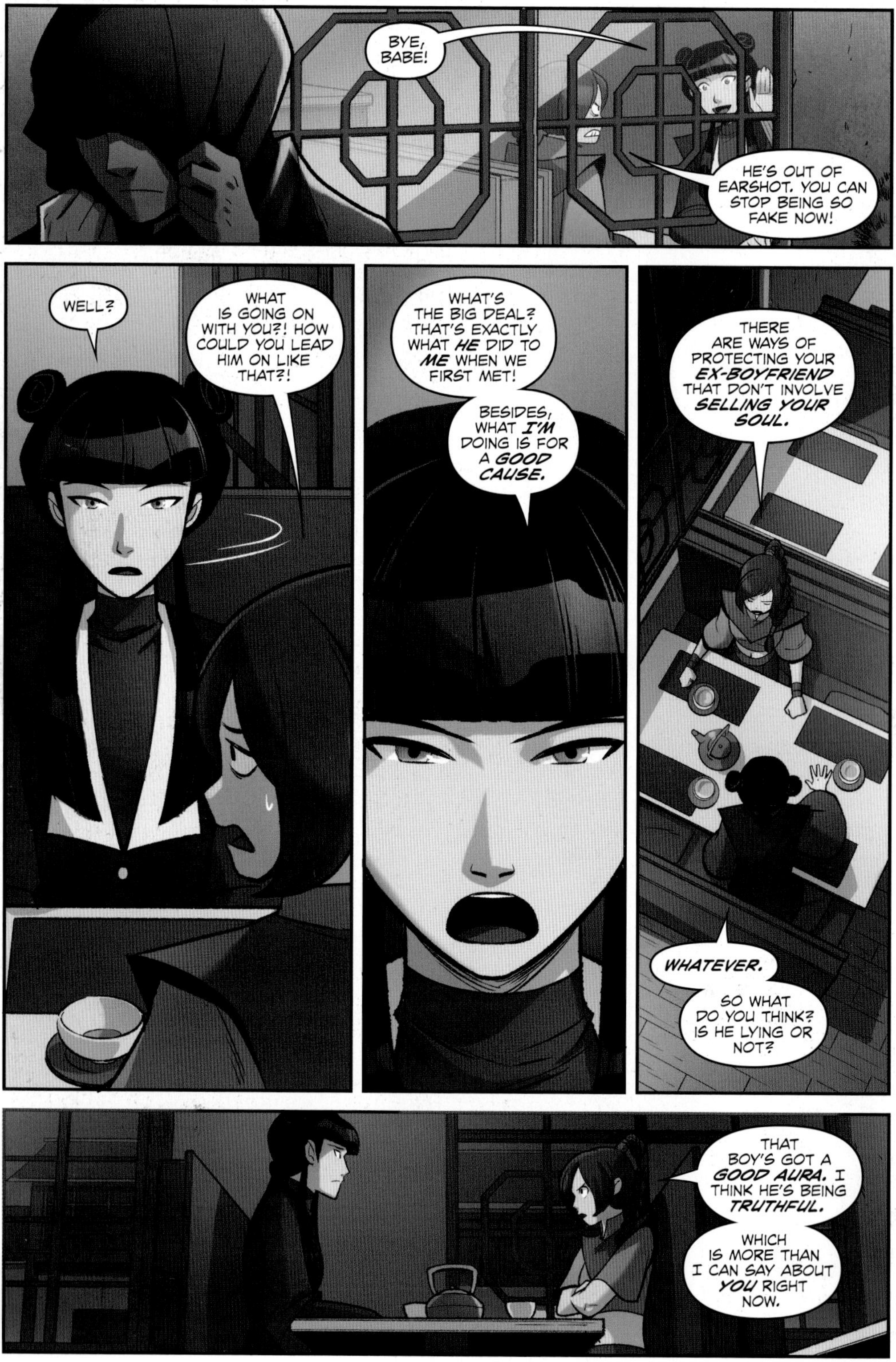
BYE, BABE!
HE'S OUT OF EARSHOT. YOU CAN STOP BEING SO FAKE NOW!
WELL?
WHAT IS GOING ON WITH YOU?! HOW COULD YOU LEAD HIM ON LIKE THAT?!
WHAT'S THE BIG DEAL? THAT'S EXACTLY WHAT HE DID TO ME WHEN WE FIRST MET!
BESIDES, WHAT I'M DOING IS FOR A GOOD CAUSE.
THERE ARE WAYS OF PROTECTING YOUR EX-BOYFRIEND THAT DON'T INVOLVE SELLING YOUR SOUL.
WHATEVER.
SO WHAT DO YOU THINK? IS HE LYING OR NOT?
THAT BOY'S GOT A GOOD AURA. I THINK HE'S BEING TRUTHFUL.
WHICH IS MORE THAN I CAN SAY ABOUT YOU RIGHT NOW.

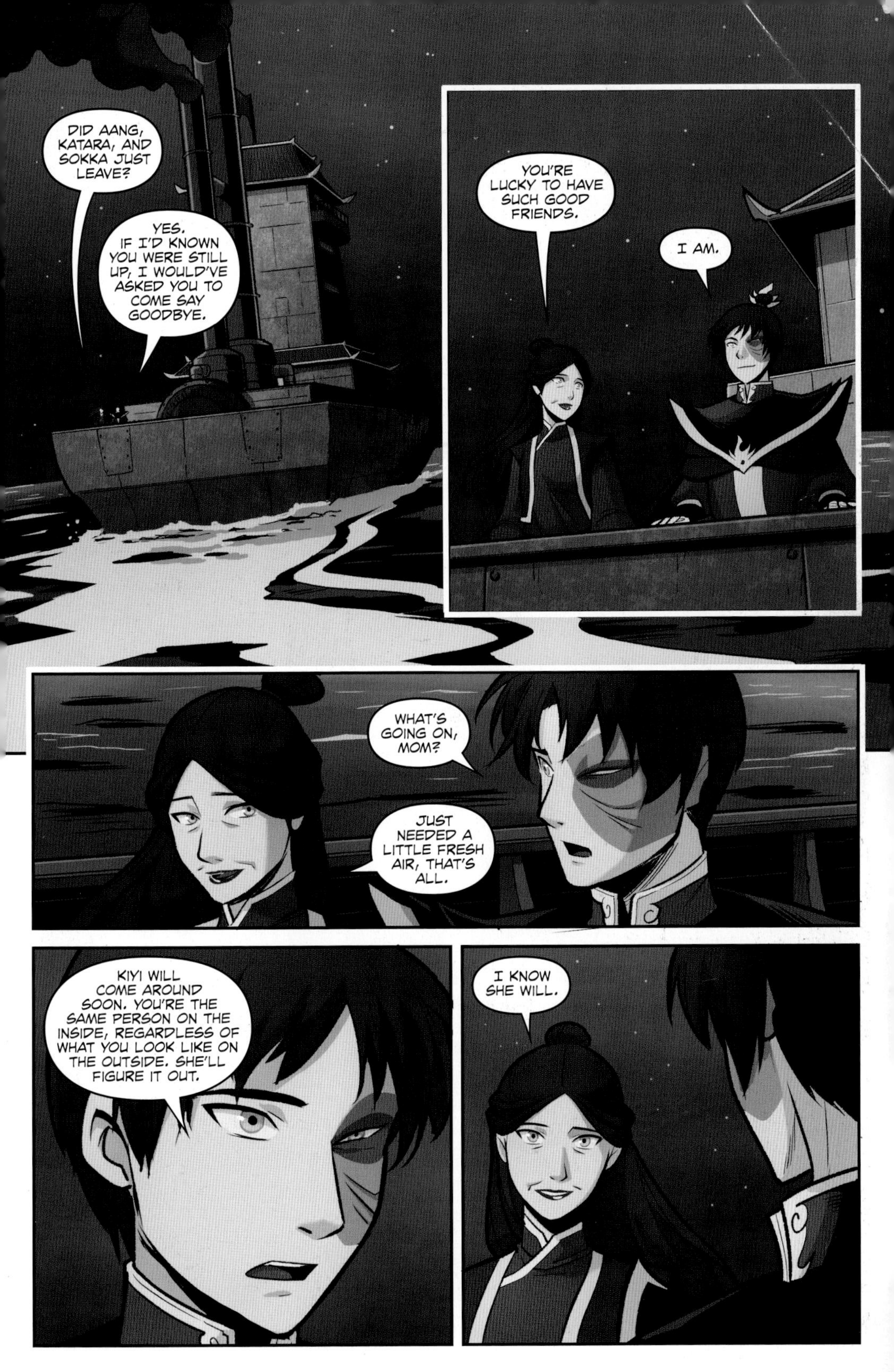
DID AANG, KATARA, AND SOKKA JUST LEAVE?
YES. IF I'D KNOWN YOU WERE STILL UP, I WOULD'VE ASKED YOU TO COME SAY GOODBYE.
YOU'RE LUCKY TO HAVE SUCH GOOD FRIENDS.
I AM.
WHAT'S GOING ON, MOM?
JUST NEEDED A LITTLE FRESH AIR, THAT'S ALL.
KIYI WILL COME AROUND SOON. YOU'RE THE SAME PERSON ON THE INSIDE, REGARDLESS OF WHAT YOU LOOK LIKE ON THE OUTSIDE. SHE'LL FIGURE IT OUT.
I KNOW SHE WILL.

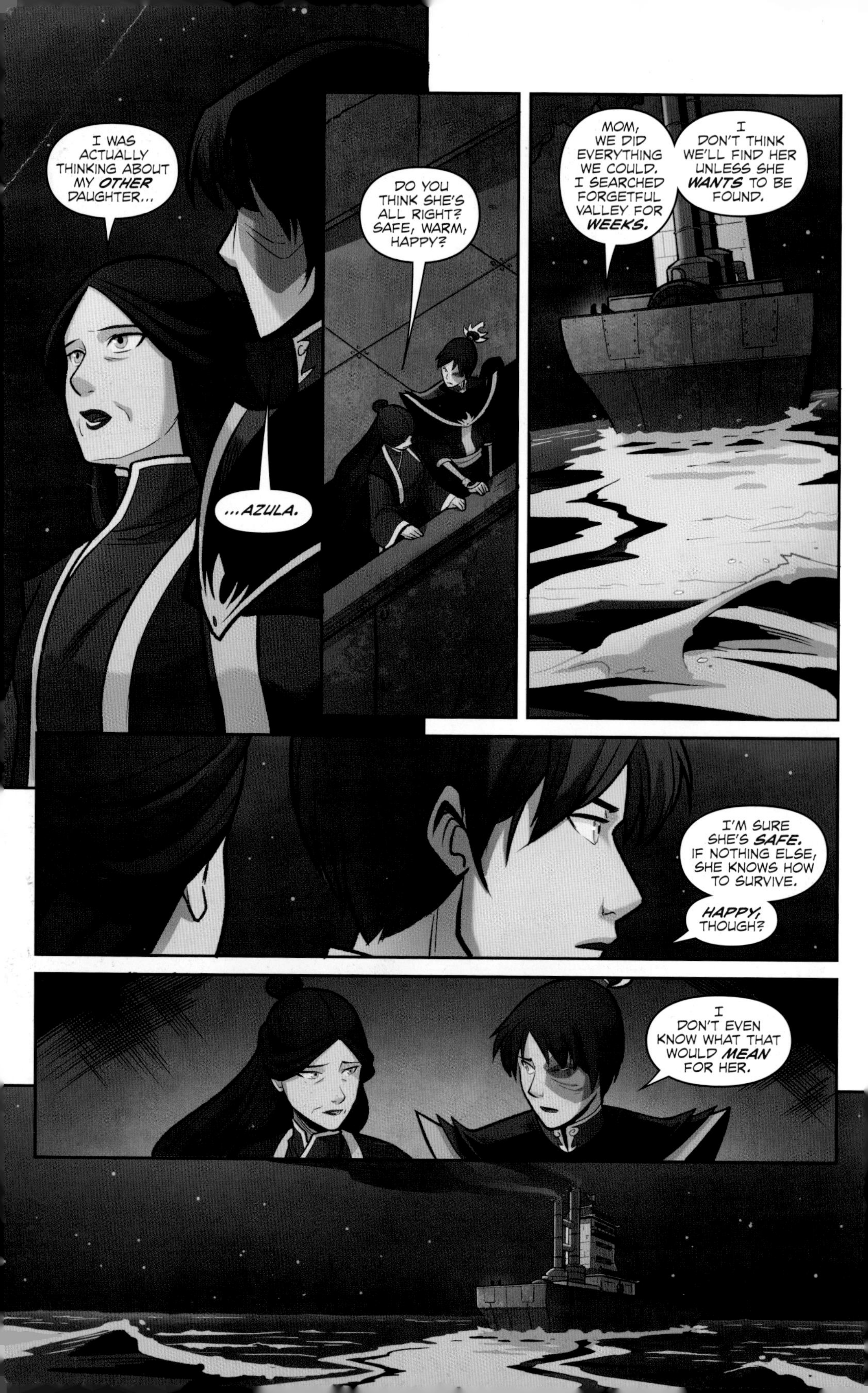
I WAS ACTUALLY THINKING ABOUT MY *OTHER* DAUGHTER...
...AZULA.
DO YOU THINK SHE'S ALL RIGHT? SAFE, WARM, HAPPY?
MOM, WE DID EVERYTHING WE COULD. I SEARCHED FORGETFUL VALLEY FOR *WEEKS.*
I DON'T THINK WE'LL FIND HER UNLESS SHE *WANTS* TO BE FOUND.
I'M SURE SHE'S *SAFE.* IF NOTHING ELSE, SHE KNOWS HOW TO SURVIVE.
HAPPY, THOUGH?
I DON'T EVEN KNOW WHAT THAT WOULD *MEAN* FOR HER.

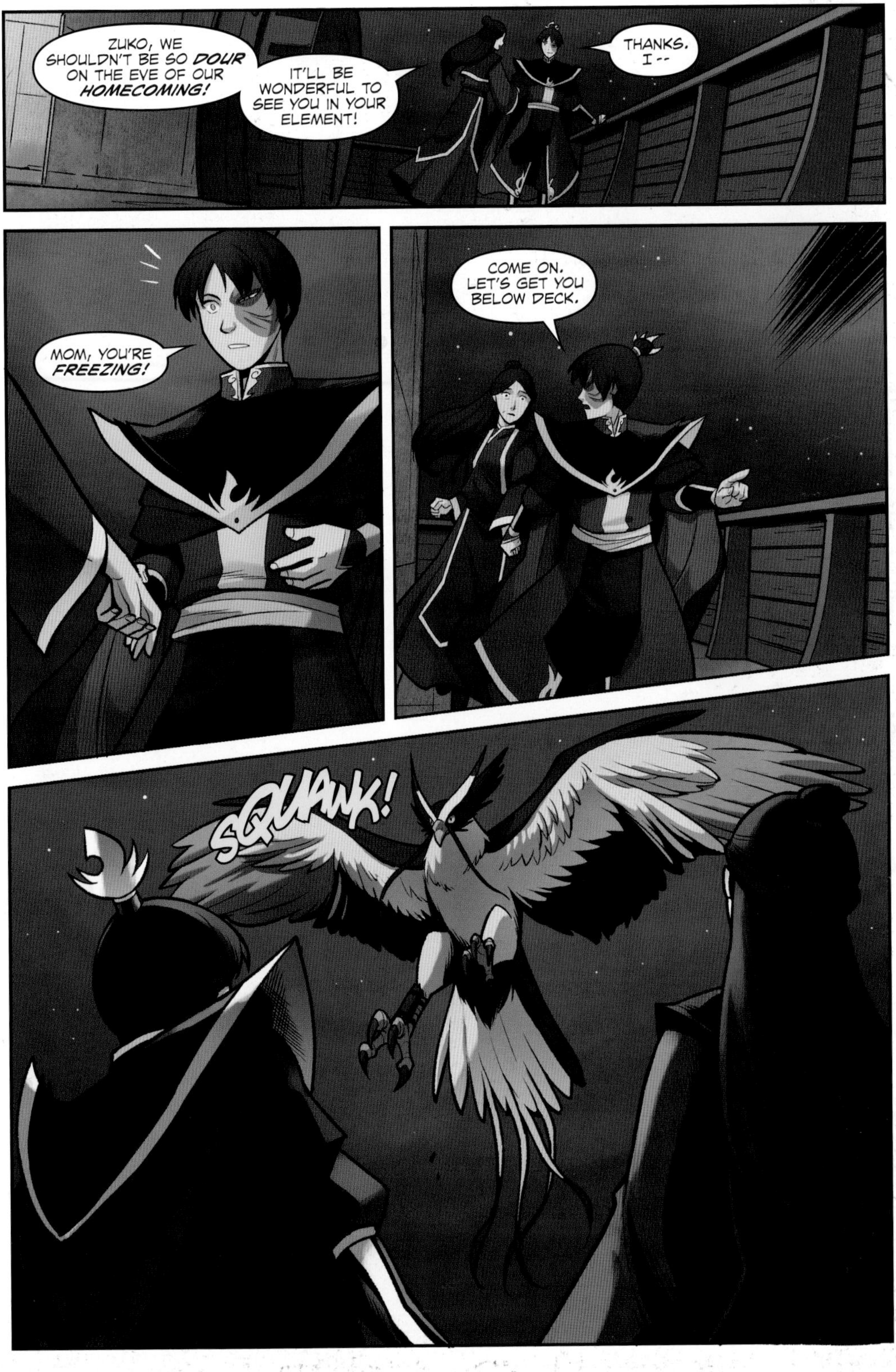
ZUKO, WE SHOULDN'T BE SO DOUR ON THE EVE OF OUR HOMECOMING!
IT'LL BE WONDERFUL TO SEE YOU IN YOUR ELEMENT!
THANKS. I --
MOM, YOU'RE FREEZING!
COME ON. LET'S GET YOU BELOW DECK.
SQUAWK!

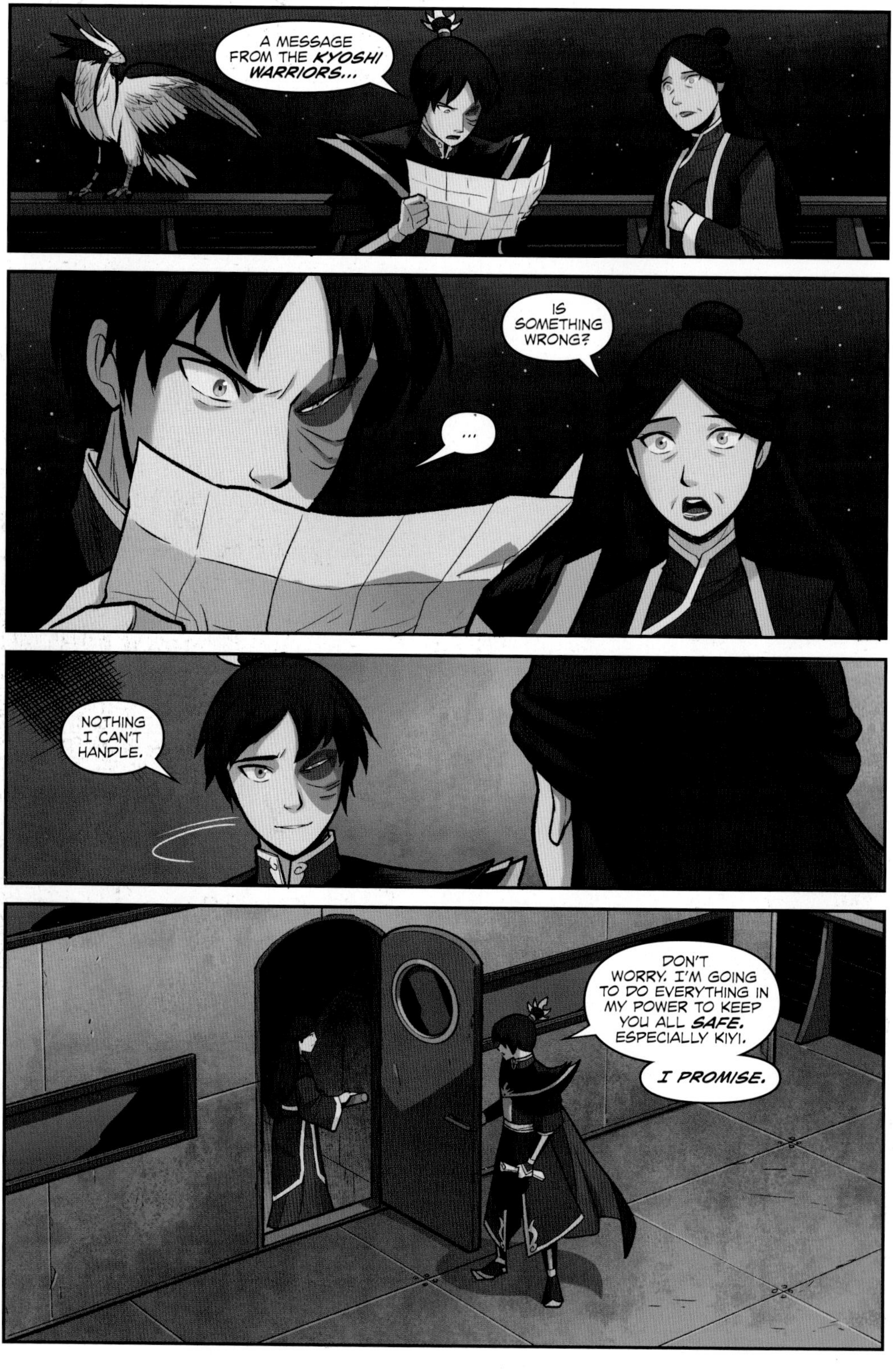
A MESSAGE FROM THE KYOSHI WARRIORS...
IS SOMETHING WRONG?
...
NOTHING I CAN'T HANDLE.
DON'T WORRY. I'M GOING TO DO EVERYTHING IN MY POWER TO KEEP YOU ALL SAFE. ESPECIALLY KIYI.
I PROMISE.

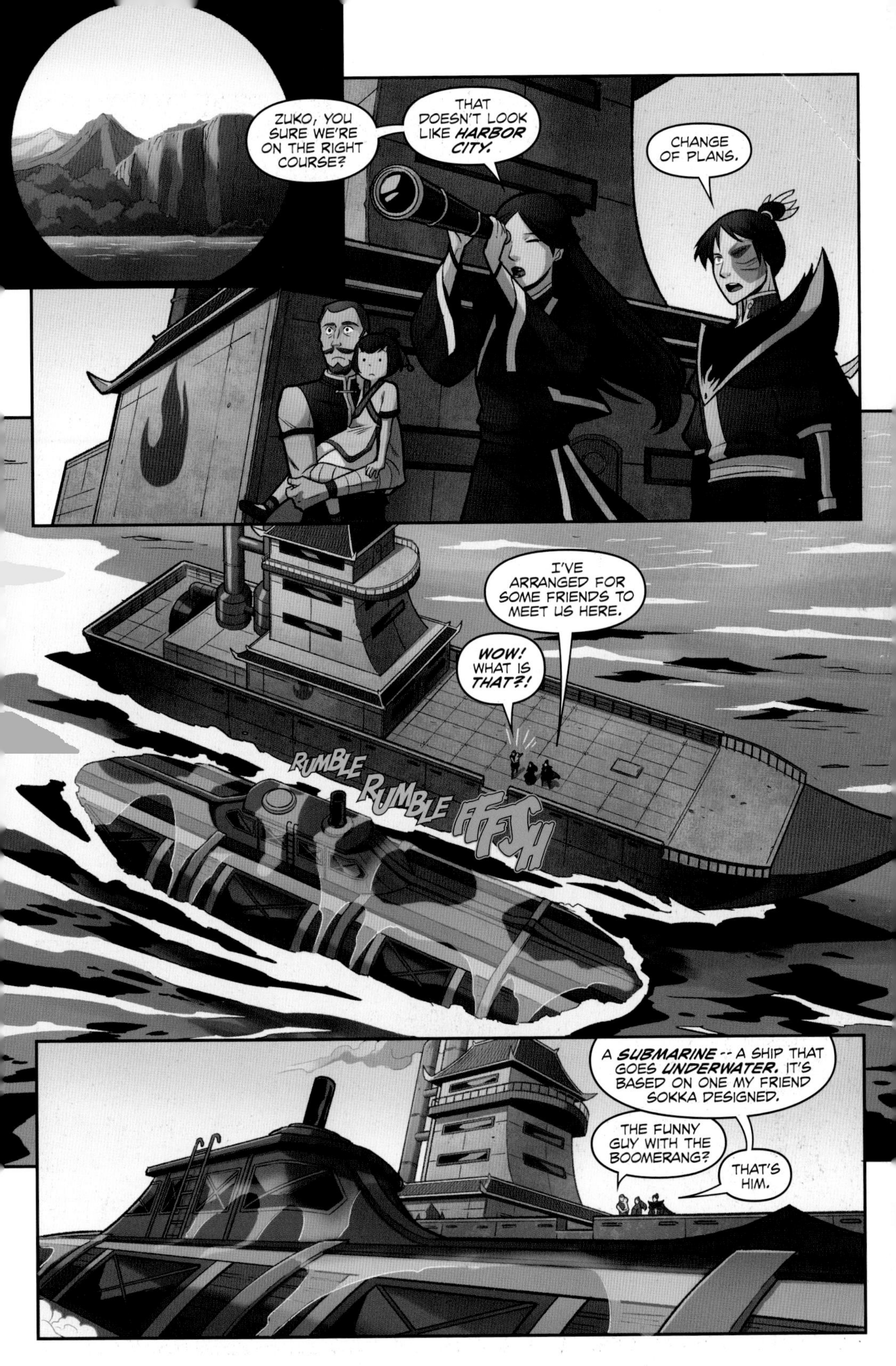
ZUKO, YOU SURE WE'RE ON THE RIGHT COURSE?
THAT DOESN'T LOOK LIKE HARBOR CITY.
CHANGE OF PLANS.
I'VE ARRANGED FOR SOME FRIENDS TO MEET US HERE.
WOW! WHAT IS THAT?!
RUMBLE RUMBLE
FFFSH
A SUBMARINE -- A SHIP THAT GOES UNDERWATER. IT'S BASED ON ONE MY FRIEND SOKKA DESIGNED.
THE FUNNY GUY WITH THE BOOMERANG?
THAT'S HIM.

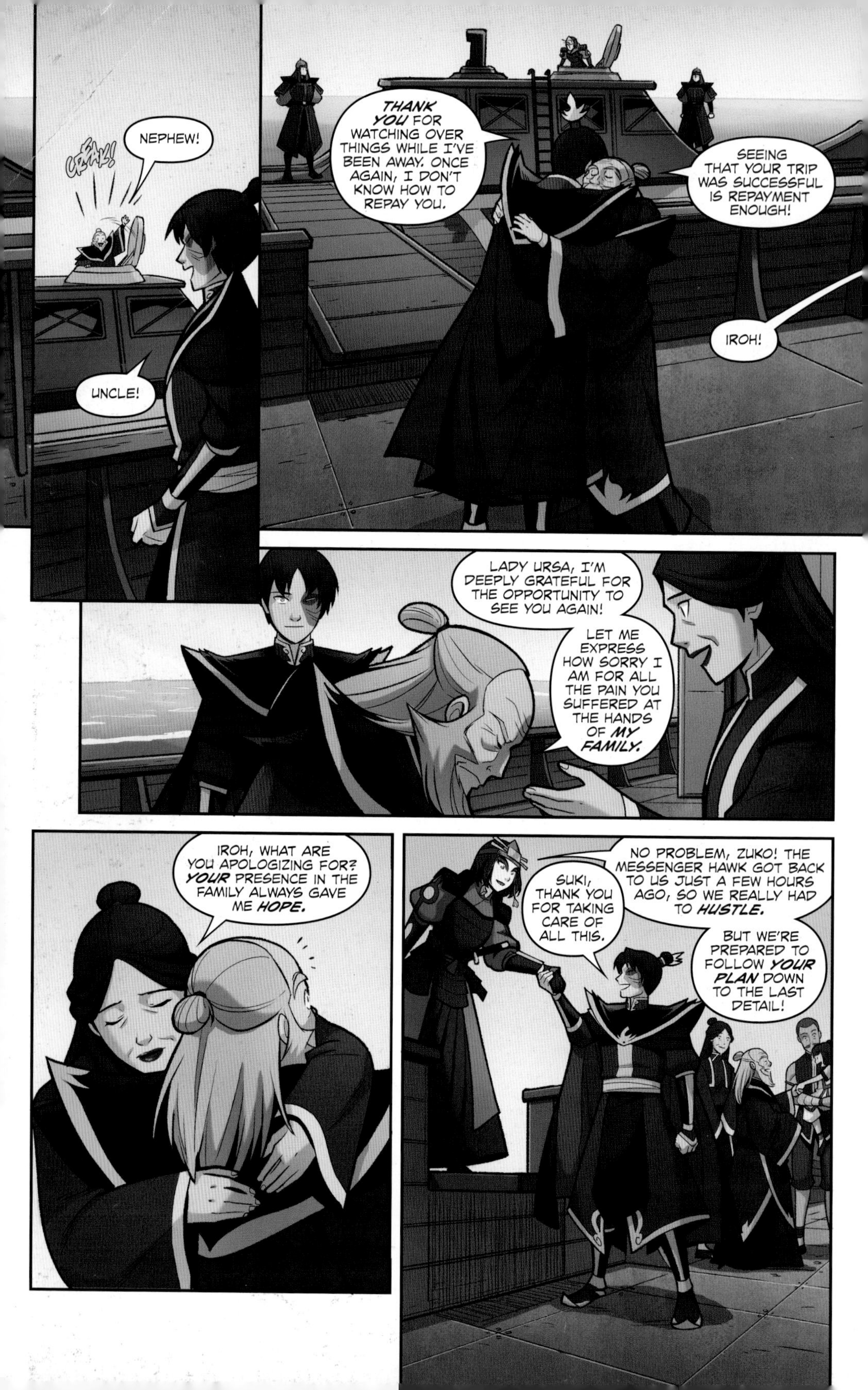
CREAK!
NEPHEW!
UNCLE!
THANK YOU FOR WATCHING OVER THINGS WHILE I'VE BEEN AWAY. ONCE AGAIN, I DON'T KNOW HOW TO REPAY YOU.
SEEING THAT YOUR TRIP WAS SUCCESSFUL IS REPAYMENT ENOUGH!
IROH!
LADY URSA, I'M DEEPLY GRATEFUL FOR THE OPPORTUNITY TO SEE YOU AGAIN!
LET ME EXPRESS HOW SORRY I AM FOR ALL THE PAIN YOU SUFFERED AT THE HANDS OF MY FAMILY.
IROH, WHAT ARE YOU APOLOGIZING FOR? YOUR PRESENCE IN THE FAMILY ALWAYS GAVE ME HOPE.
SUKI, THANK YOU FOR TAKING CARE OF ALL THIS.
NO PROBLEM, ZUKO! THE MESSENGER HAWK GOT BACK TO US JUST A FEW HOURS AGO, SO WE REALLY HAD TO HUSTLE.
BUT WE'RE PREPARED TO FOLLOW YOUR PLAN DOWN TO THE LAST DETAIL!

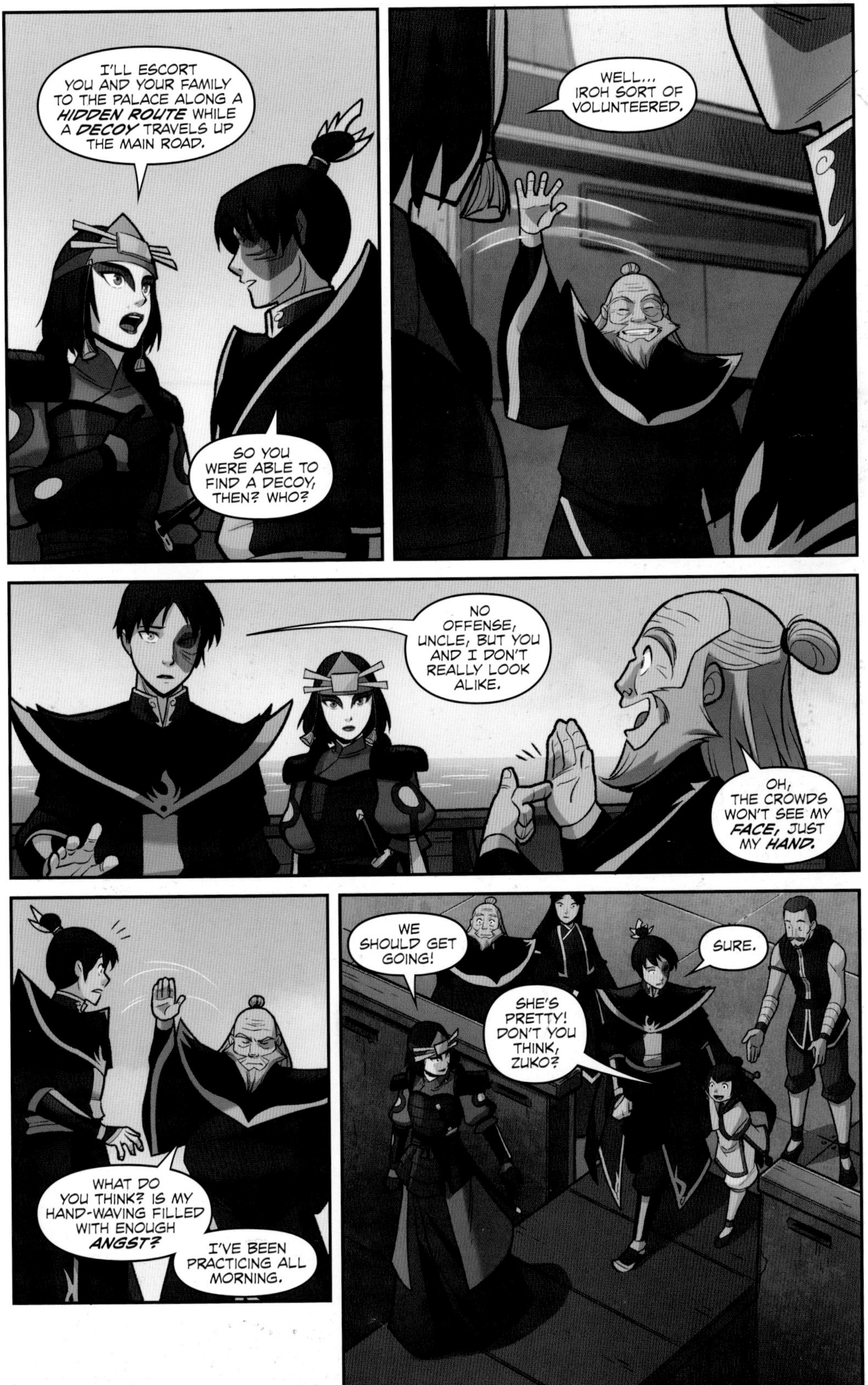
I'LL ESCORT YOU AND YOUR FAMILY TO THE PALACE ALONG A ***HIDDEN ROUTE*** WHILE A ***DECOY*** TRAVELS UP THE MAIN ROAD.
SO YOU WERE ABLE TO FIND A DECOY, THEN? WHO?
WELL... IROH SORT OF VOLUNTEERED.
NO OFFENSE, UNCLE, BUT YOU AND I DON'T REALLY LOOK ALIKE.
OH, THE CROWDS WON'T SEE MY ***FACE,*** JUST MY ***HAND.***
WHAT DO YOU THINK? IS MY HAND-WAVING FILLED WITH ENOUGH ***ANGST?***
I'VE BEEN PRACTICING ALL MORNING.
WE SHOULD GET GOING!
SURE.
SHE'S PRETTY! DON'T YOU THINK, ZUKO?

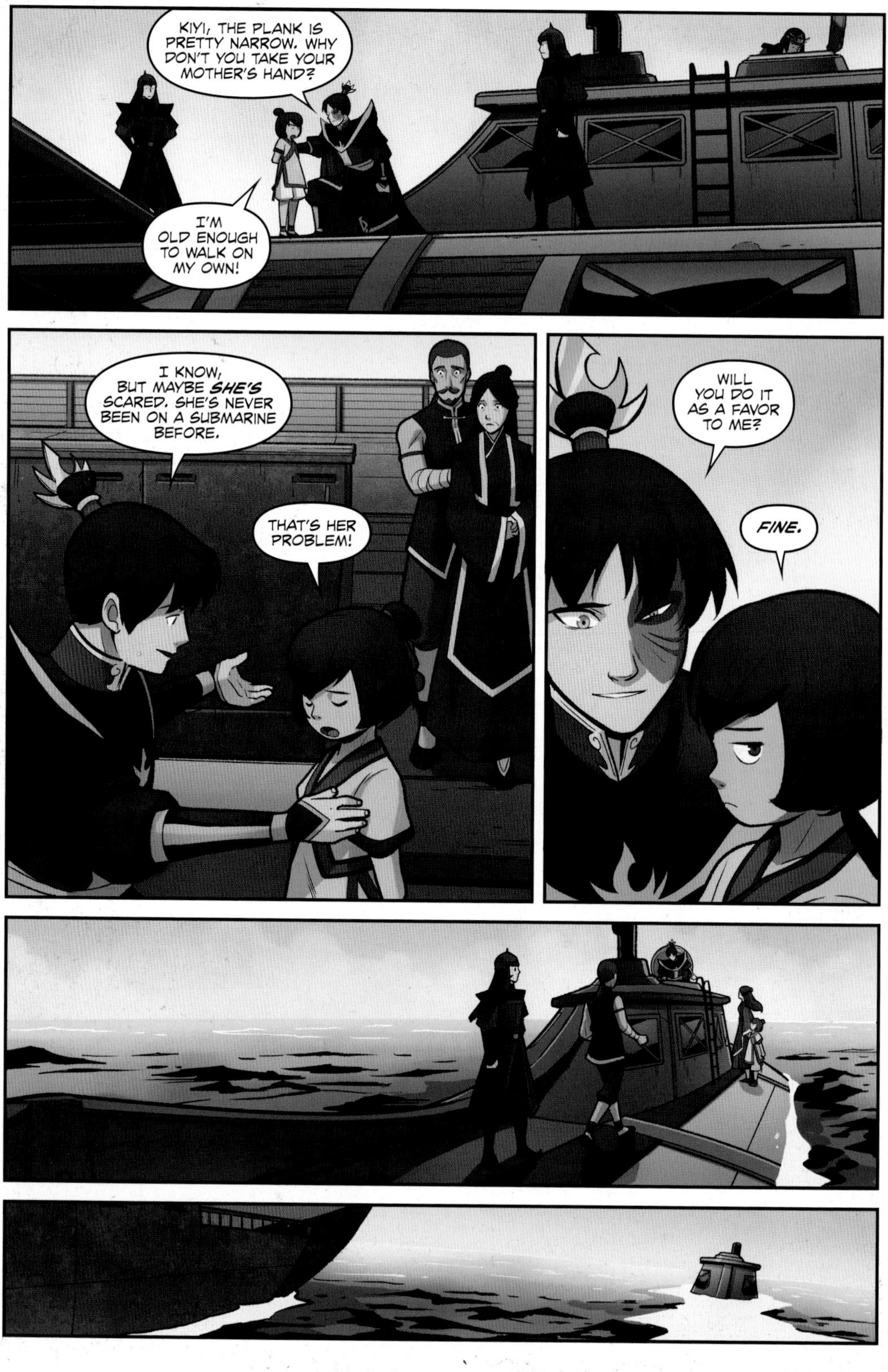
KIYI, THE PLANK IS PRETTY NARROW. WHY DON'T YOU TAKE YOUR MOTHER'S HAND?
I'M OLD ENOUGH TO WALK ON MY OWN!
I KNOW, BUT MAYBE ***SHE'S*** SCARED. SHE'S NEVER BEEN ON A SUBMARINE BEFORE.
THAT'S HER PROBLEM!
WILL YOU DO IT AS A FAVOR TO ME?
FINE.

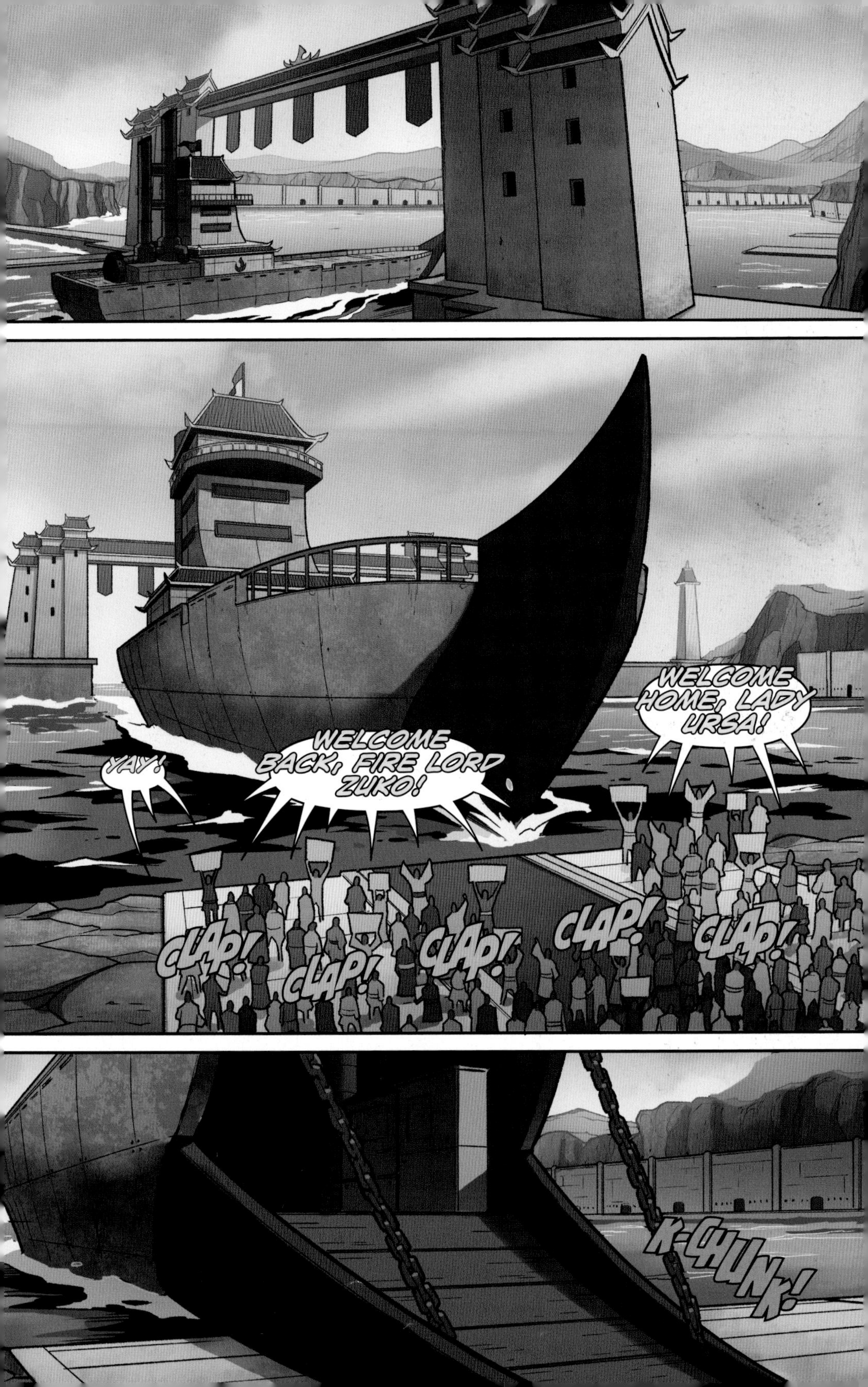
YAY!
WELCOME BACK, FIRE LORD ZUKO!
WELCOME HOME, LADY URSA!
CLAP! CLAP! CLAP! CLAP! CLAP!
K-CHUNK!

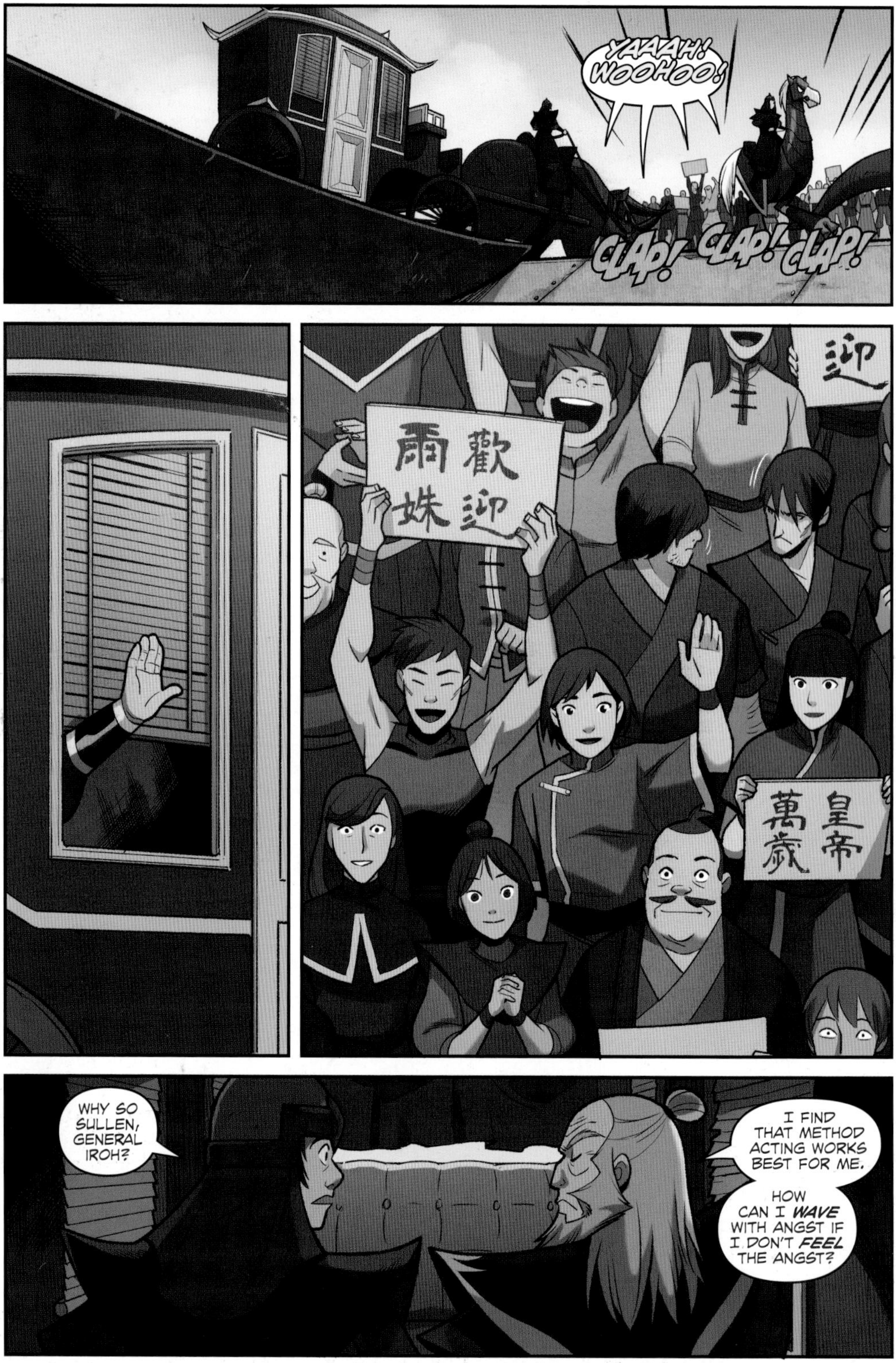
YAAAAH! WOOHOO!
CLAP! CLAP! CLAP!
歡迎雨姝
迎
皇帝萬歲
WHY SO SULLEN, GENERAL IROH?
I FIND THAT METHOD ACTING WORKS BEST FOR ME.
HOW CAN I ***WAVE*** WITH ANGST IF I DON'T ***FEEL*** THE ANGST?

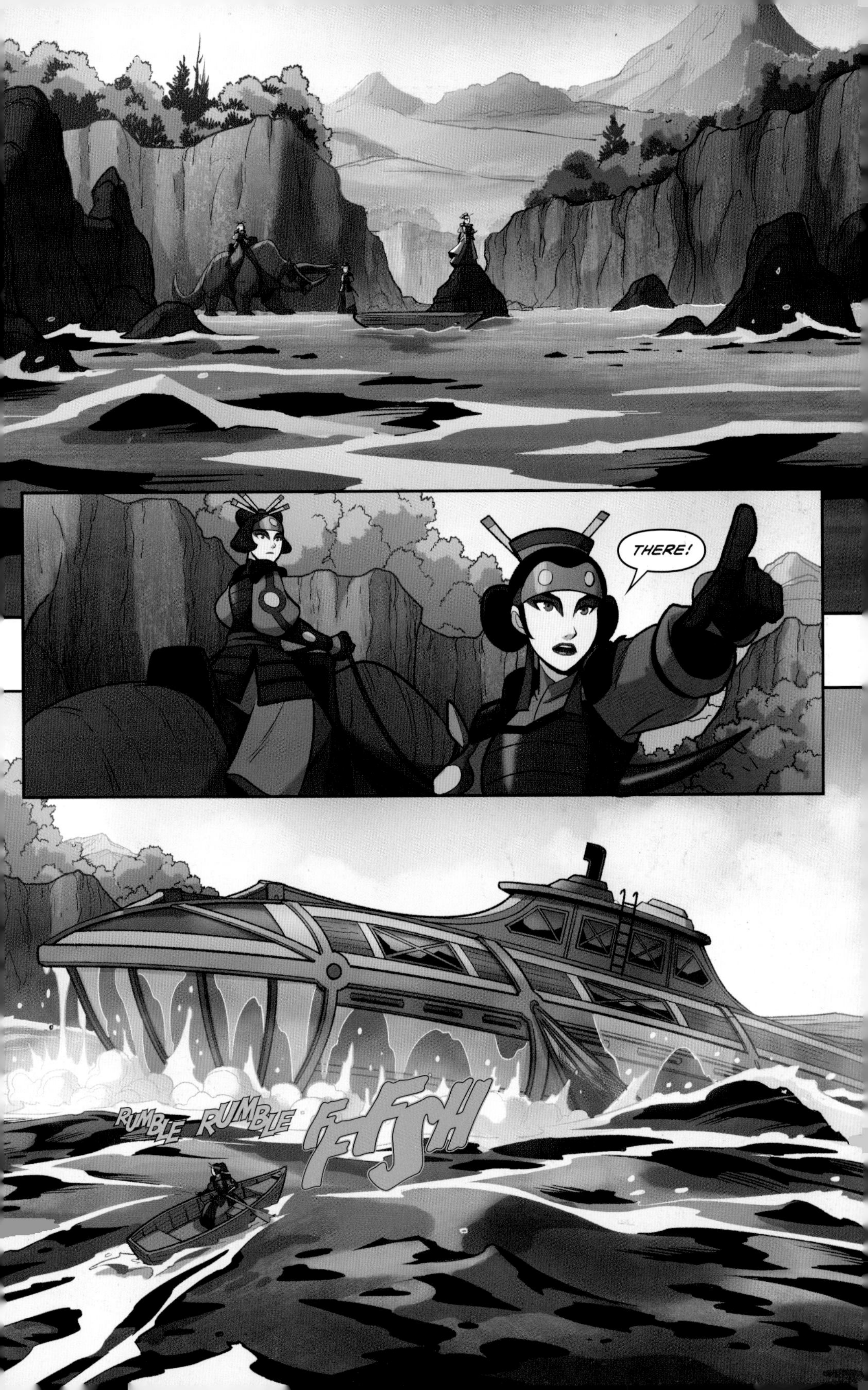
THERE!
RUMBLE RUMBLE
FFSH

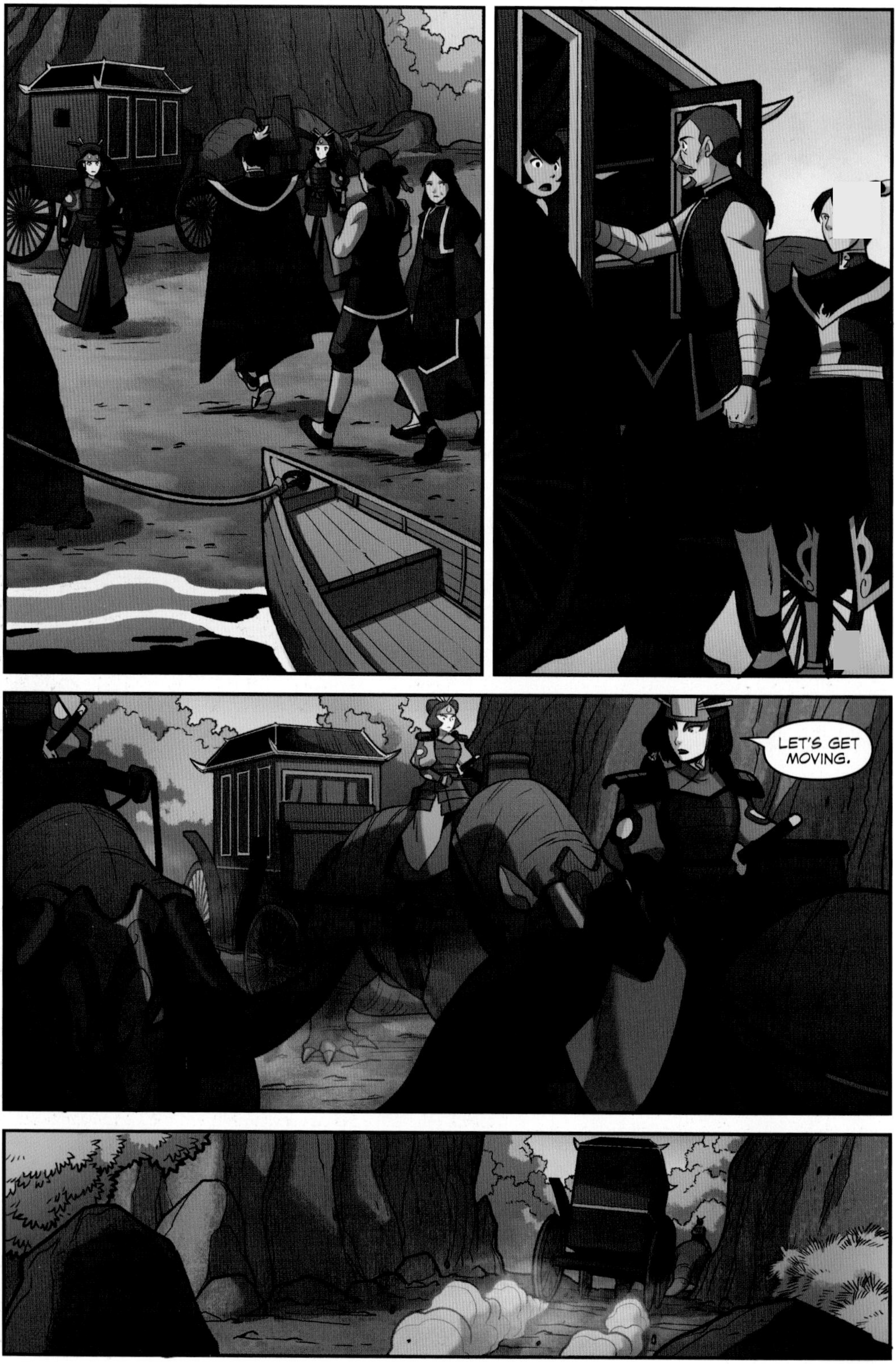
LET'S GET MOVING.

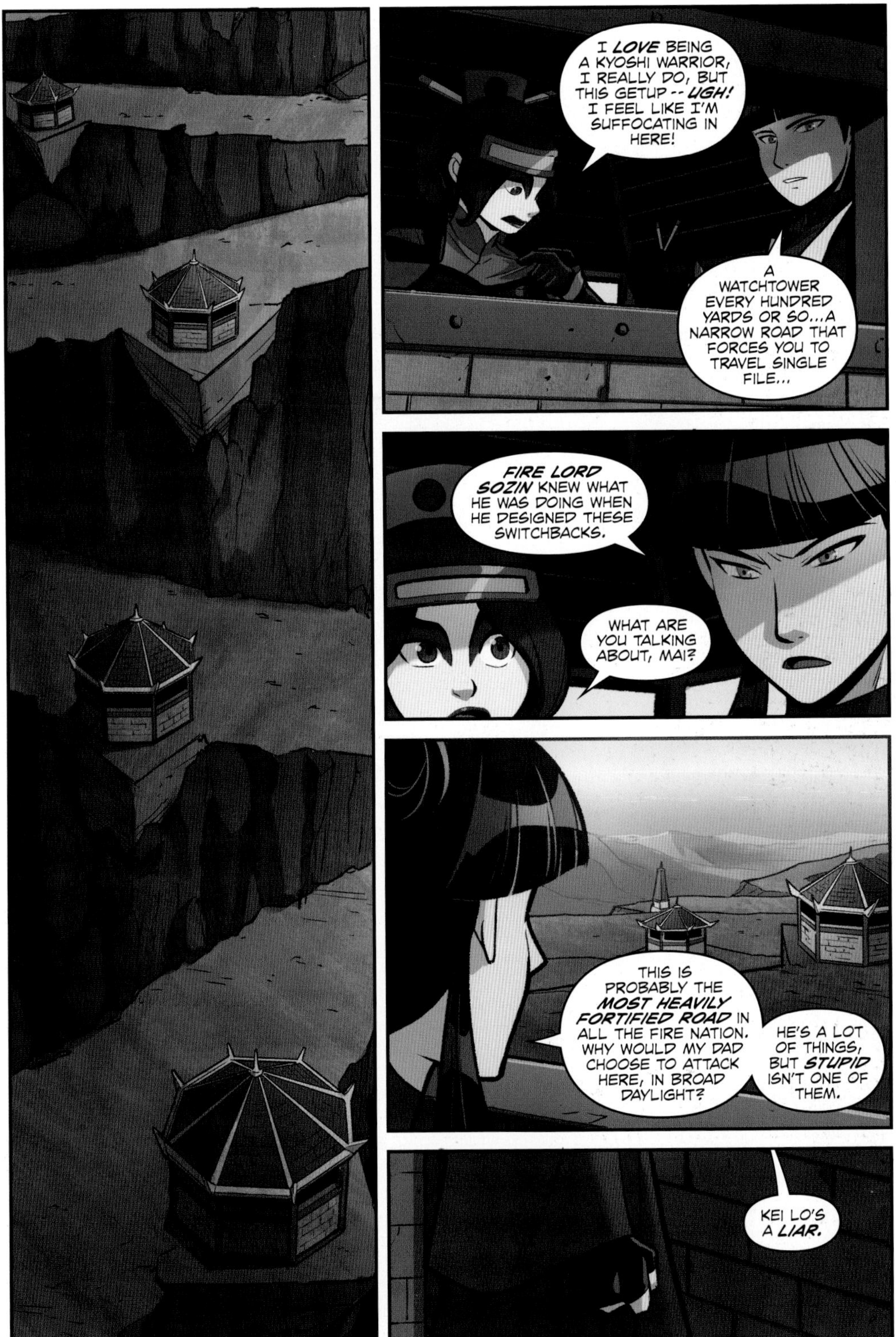
I LOVE BEING A KYOSHI WARRIOR, I REALLY DO, BUT THIS GETUP -- UGH! I FEEL LIKE I'M SUFFOCATING IN HERE!
A WATCHTOWER EVERY HUNDRED YARDS OR SO...A NARROW ROAD THAT FORCES YOU TO TRAVEL SINGLE FILE...
FIRE LORD SOZIN KNEW WHAT HE WAS DOING WHEN HE DESIGNED THESE SWITCHBACKS.
WHAT ARE YOU TALKING ABOUT, MAI?
THIS IS PROBABLY THE MOST HEAVILY FORTIFIED ROAD IN ALL THE FIRE NATION. WHY WOULD MY DAD CHOOSE TO ATTACK HERE, IN BROAD DAYLIGHT?
HE'S A LOT OF THINGS, BUT STUPID ISN'T ONE OF THEM.
KEI LO'S A LIAR.

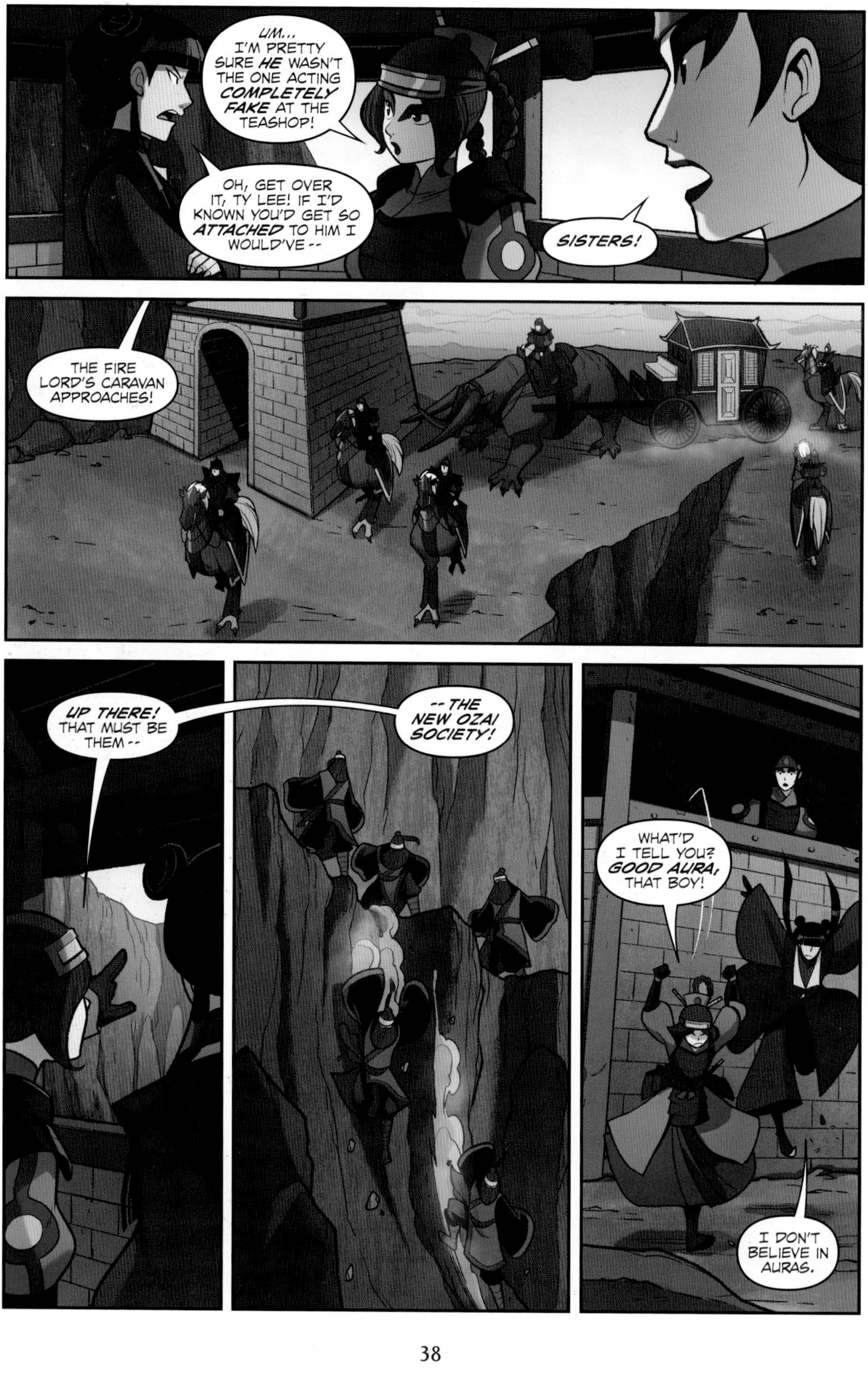
UM...
I'M PRETTY SURE HE WASN'T THE ONE ACTING COMPLETELY FAKE AT THE TEASHOP!
OH, GET OVER IT, TY LEE! IF I'D KNOWN YOU'D GET SO ATTACHED TO HIM I WOULD'VE --
SISTERS!
THE FIRE LORD'S CARAVAN APPROACHES!
UP THERE! THAT MUST BE THEM --
-- THE NEW OZAI SOCIETY!
WHAT'D I TELL YOU? GOOD AURA, THAT BOY!
I DON'T BELIEVE IN AURAS.

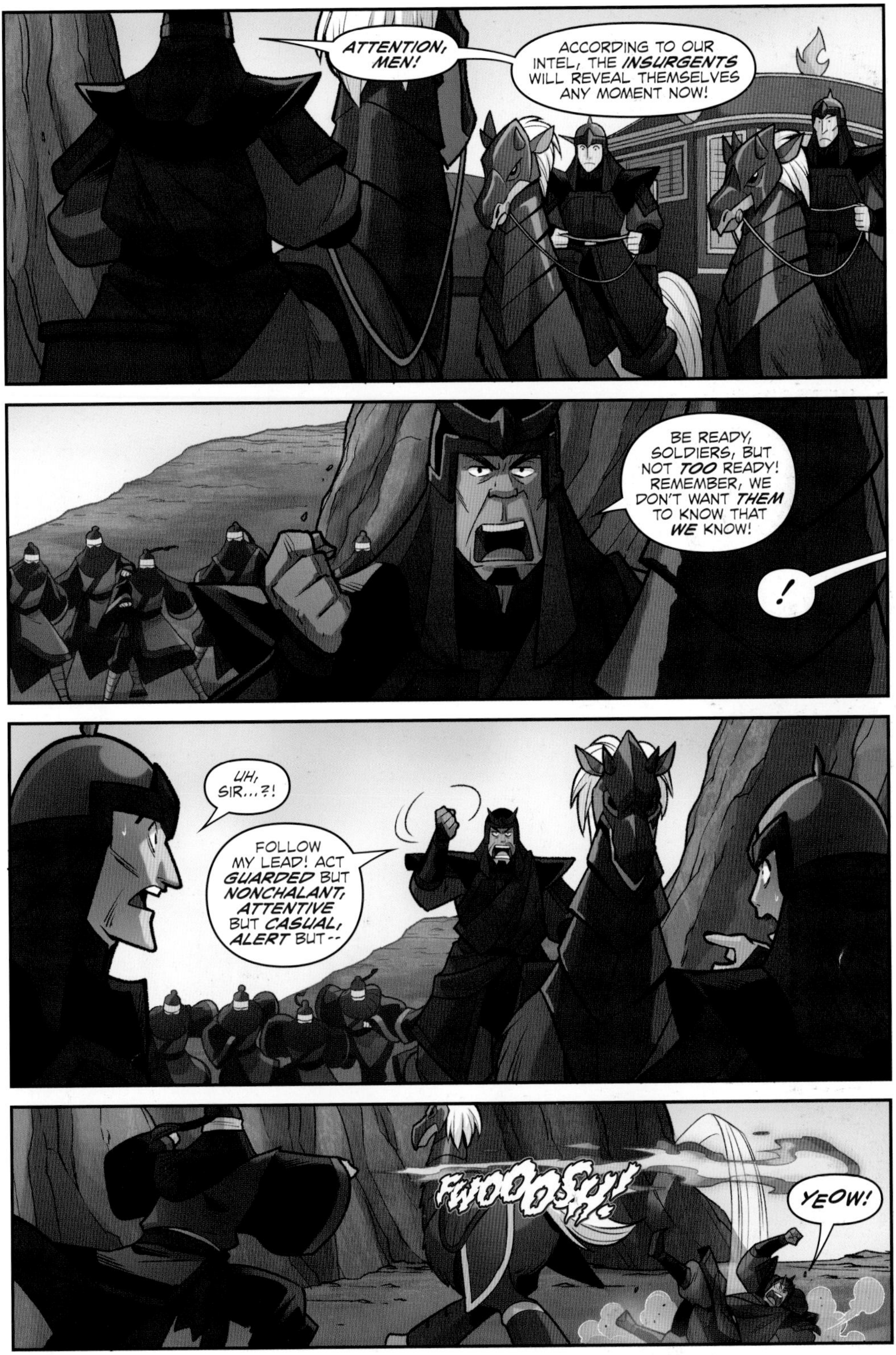
ATTENTION, MEN!
ACCORDING TO OUR INTEL, THE INSURGENTS WILL REVEAL THEMSELVES ANY MOMENT NOW!
BE READY, SOLDIERS, BUT NOT TOO READY! REMEMBER, WE DON'T WANT THEM TO KNOW THAT WE KNOW!
!
UH, SIR...?!
FOLLOW MY LEAD! ACT GUARDED BUT NONCHALANT, ATTENTIVE BUT CASUAL, ALERT BUT--
FWOOOSH!
YEOW!

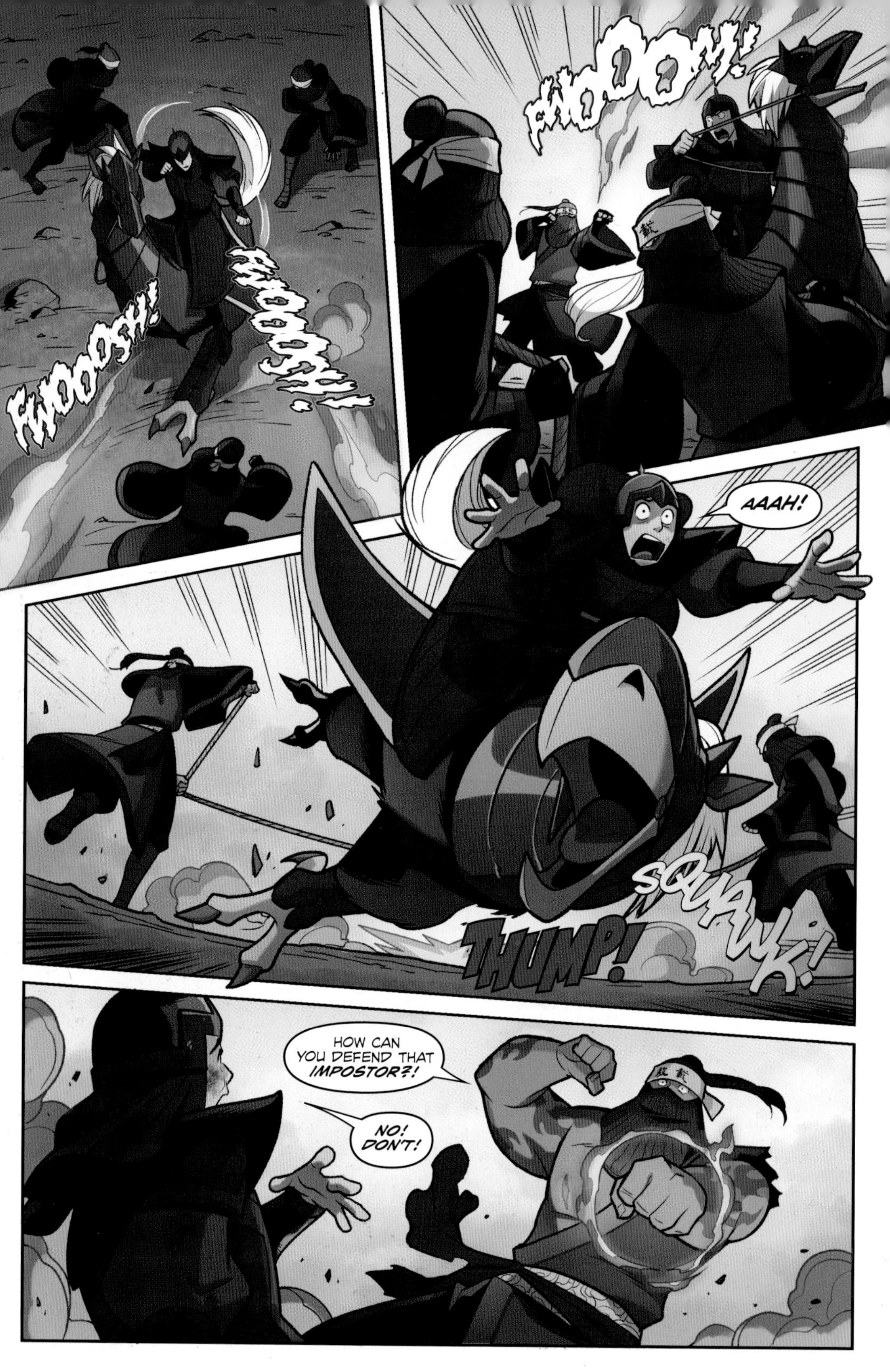
FWOOOSH!
FWOOOSH!
FWOOOM!
AAAH!
SQUAWK!
THUMP!
HOW CAN YOU DEFEND THAT *IMPOSTOR?!*
NO! DON'T!

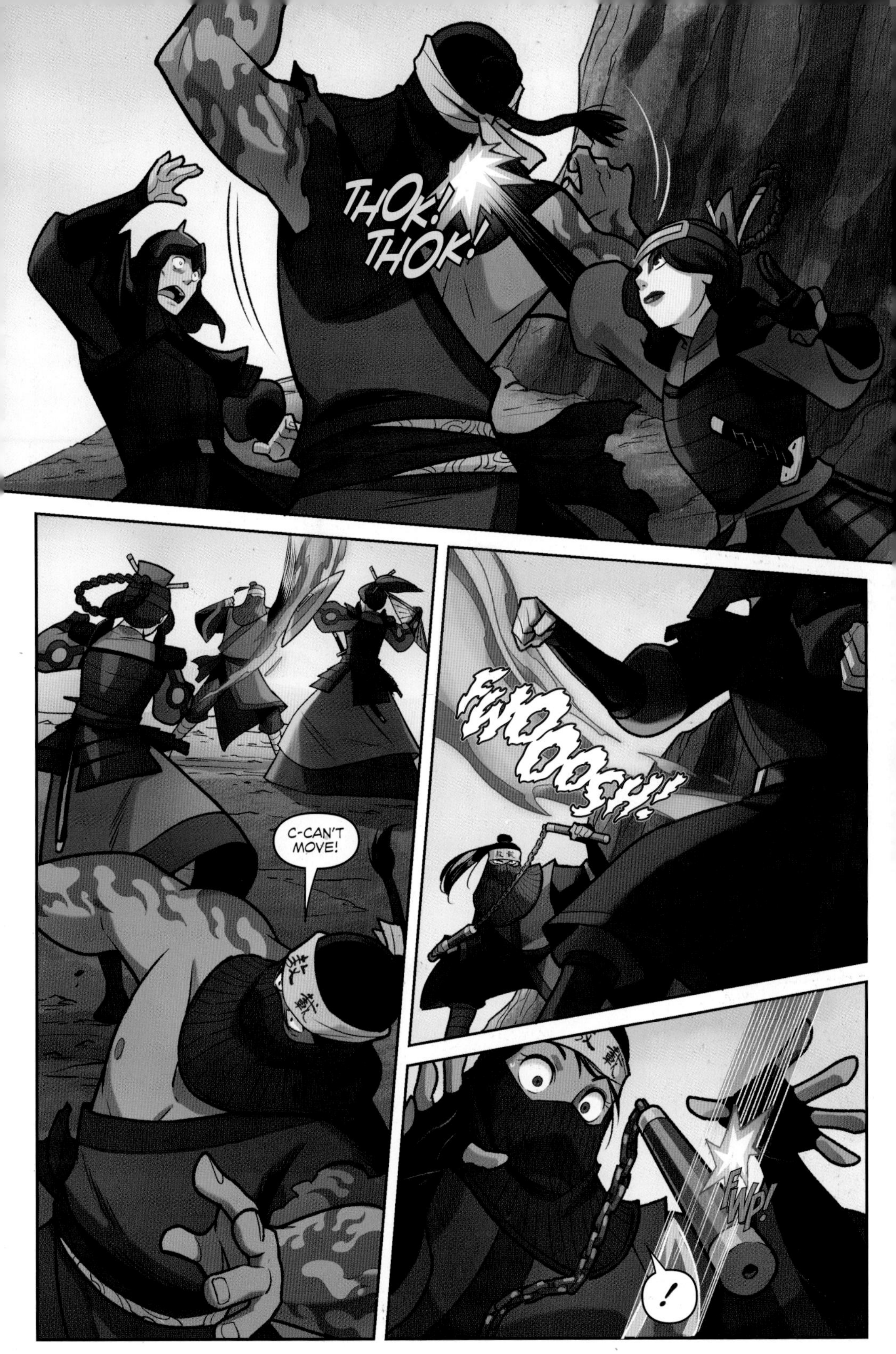
THOK! THOK!
C-CAN'T MOVE!
FWOOOSH!
FWP!
!

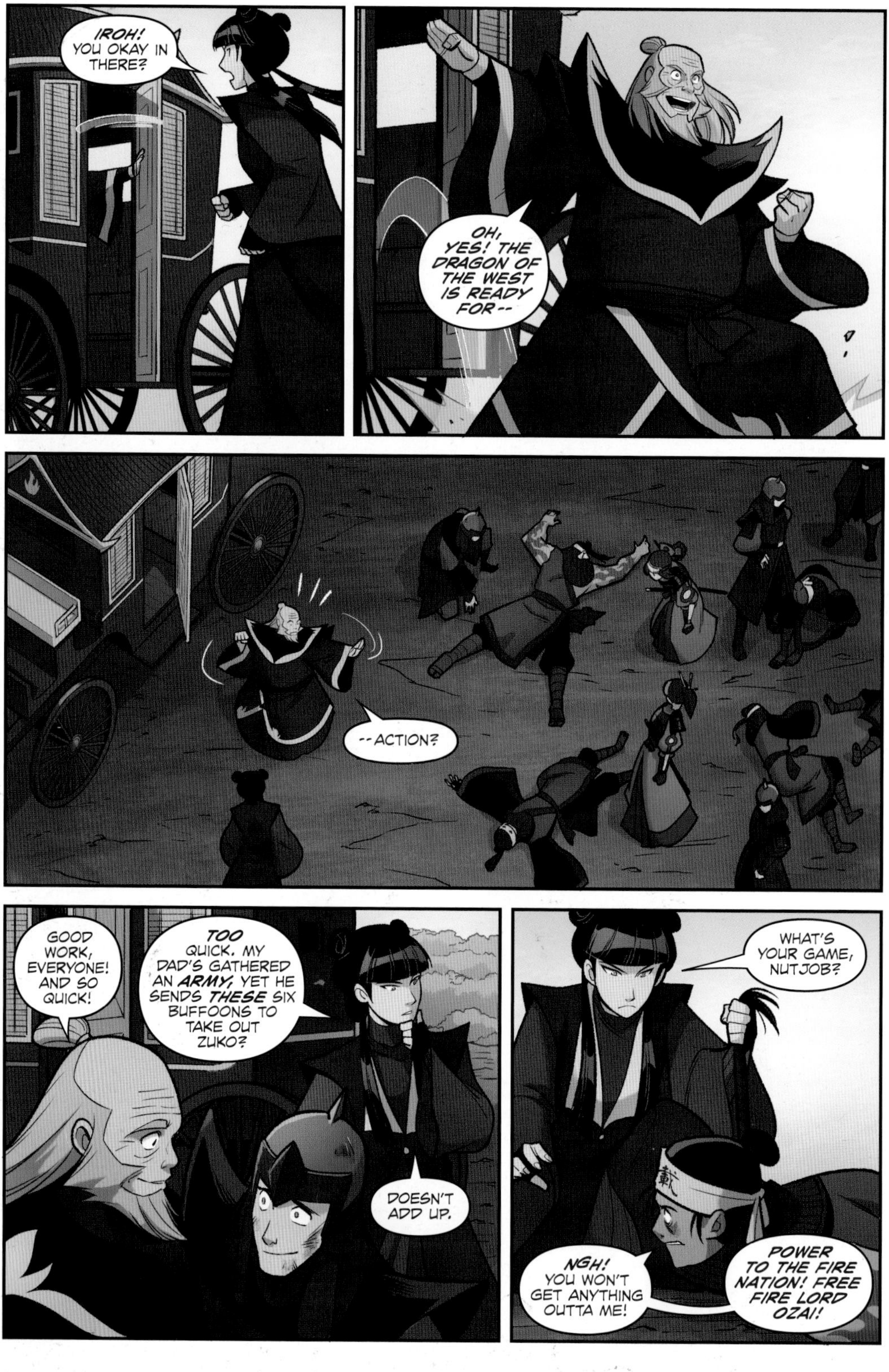
IROH! YOU OKAY IN THERE?
OH, YES! THE DRAGON OF THE WEST IS READY FOR--
--ACTION?
GOOD WORK, EVERYONE! AND SO QUICK!
TOO QUICK. MY DAD'S GATHERED AN ARMY, YET HE SENDS THESE SIX BUFFOONS TO TAKE OUT ZUKO?
DOESN'T ADD UP.
WHAT'S YOUR GAME, NUTJOB?
NGH! YOU WON'T GET ANYTHING OUTTA ME!
POWER TO THE FIRE NATION! FREE FIRE LORD OZAI!

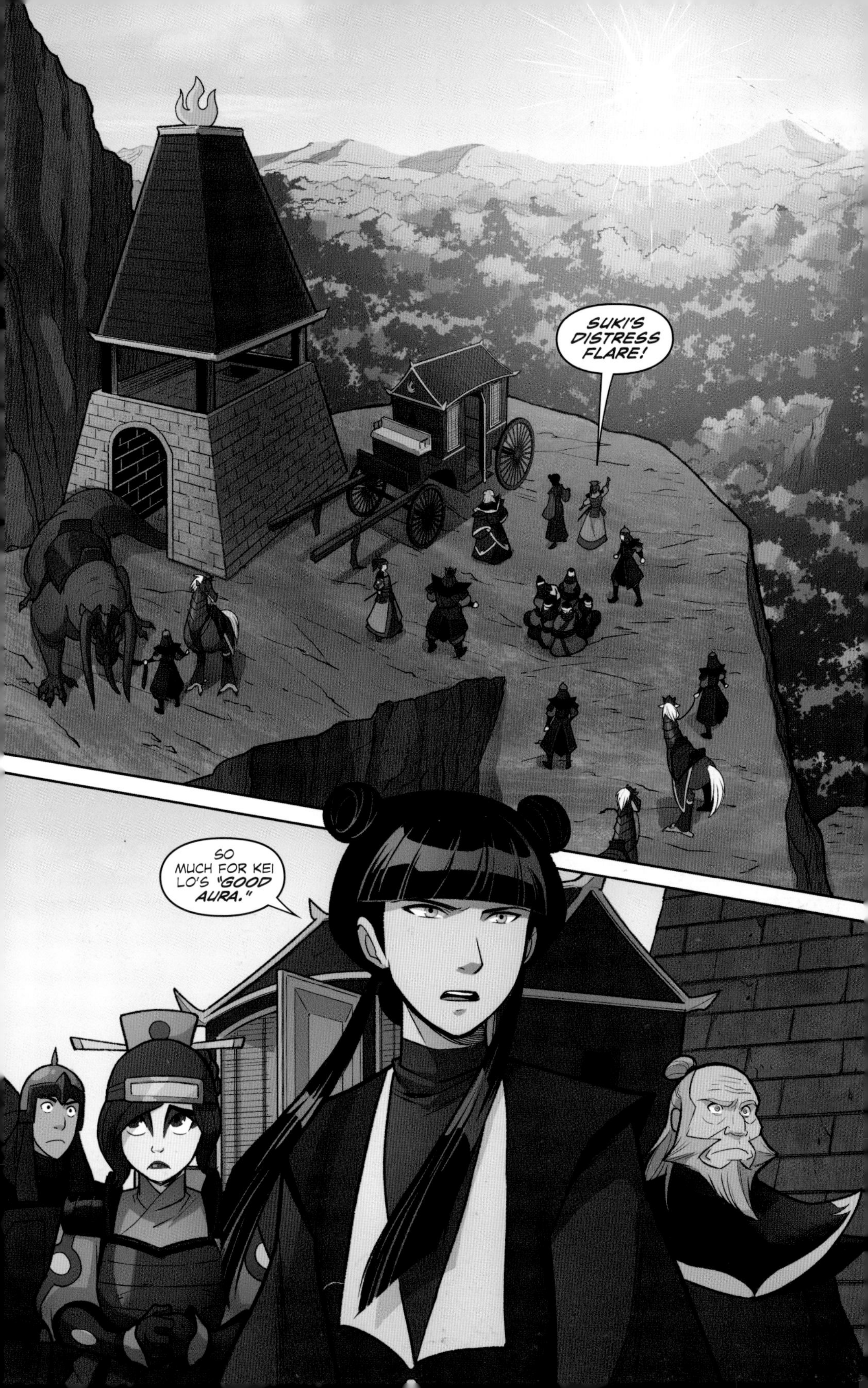
SUKI'S DISTRESS FLARE!
SO MUCH FOR KEI LO'S "GOOD AURA."

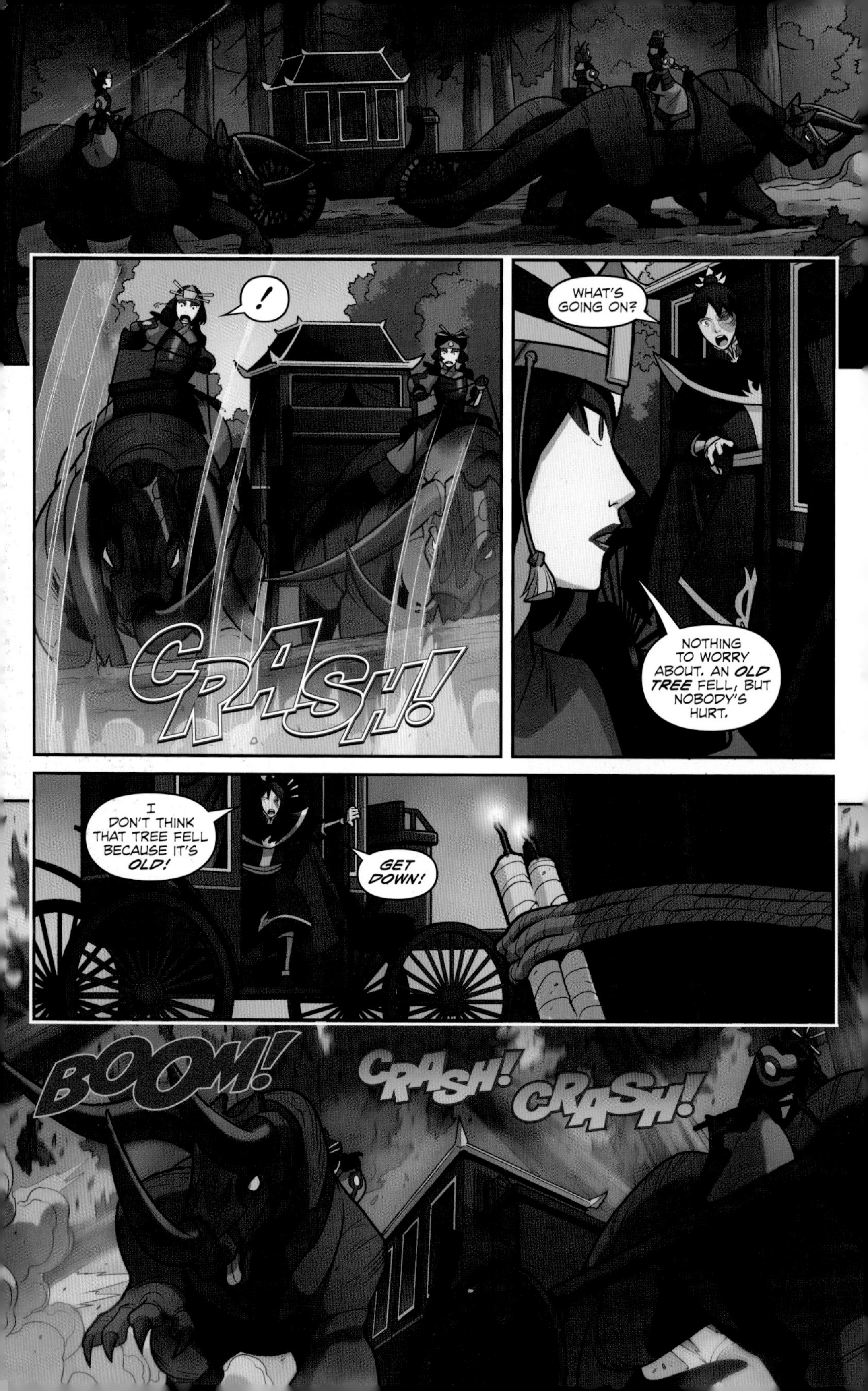
!
CRASH!
WHAT'S GOING ON?
NOTHING TO WORRY ABOUT. AN OLD TREE FELL, BUT NOBODY'S HURT.
I DON'T THINK THAT TREE FELL BECAUSE IT'S OLD!
GET DOWN!
BOOM!
CRASH! CRASH!

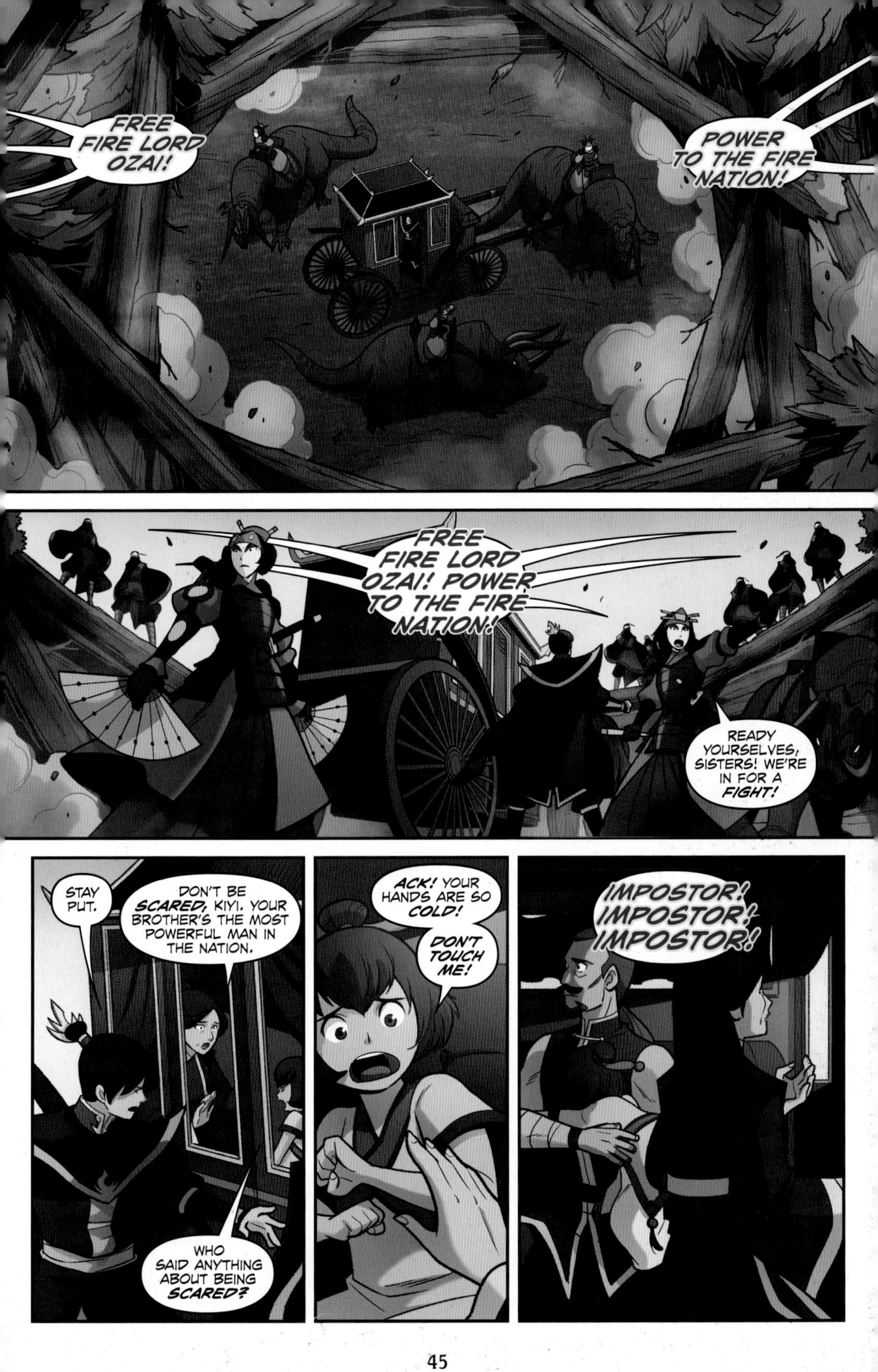
FREE FIRE LORD OZAI!
POWER TO THE FIRE NATION!
FREE FIRE LORD OZAI! POWER TO THE FIRE NATION!
READY YOURSELVES, SISTERS! WE'RE IN FOR A FIGHT!
STAY PUT.
DON'T BE SCARED, KIYI. YOUR BROTHER'S THE MOST POWERFUL MAN IN THE NATION.
WHO SAID ANYTHING ABOUT BEING SCARED?
ACK! YOUR HANDS ARE SO COLD!
DON'T TOUCH ME!
IMPOSTOR! IMPOSTOR! IMPOSTOR!

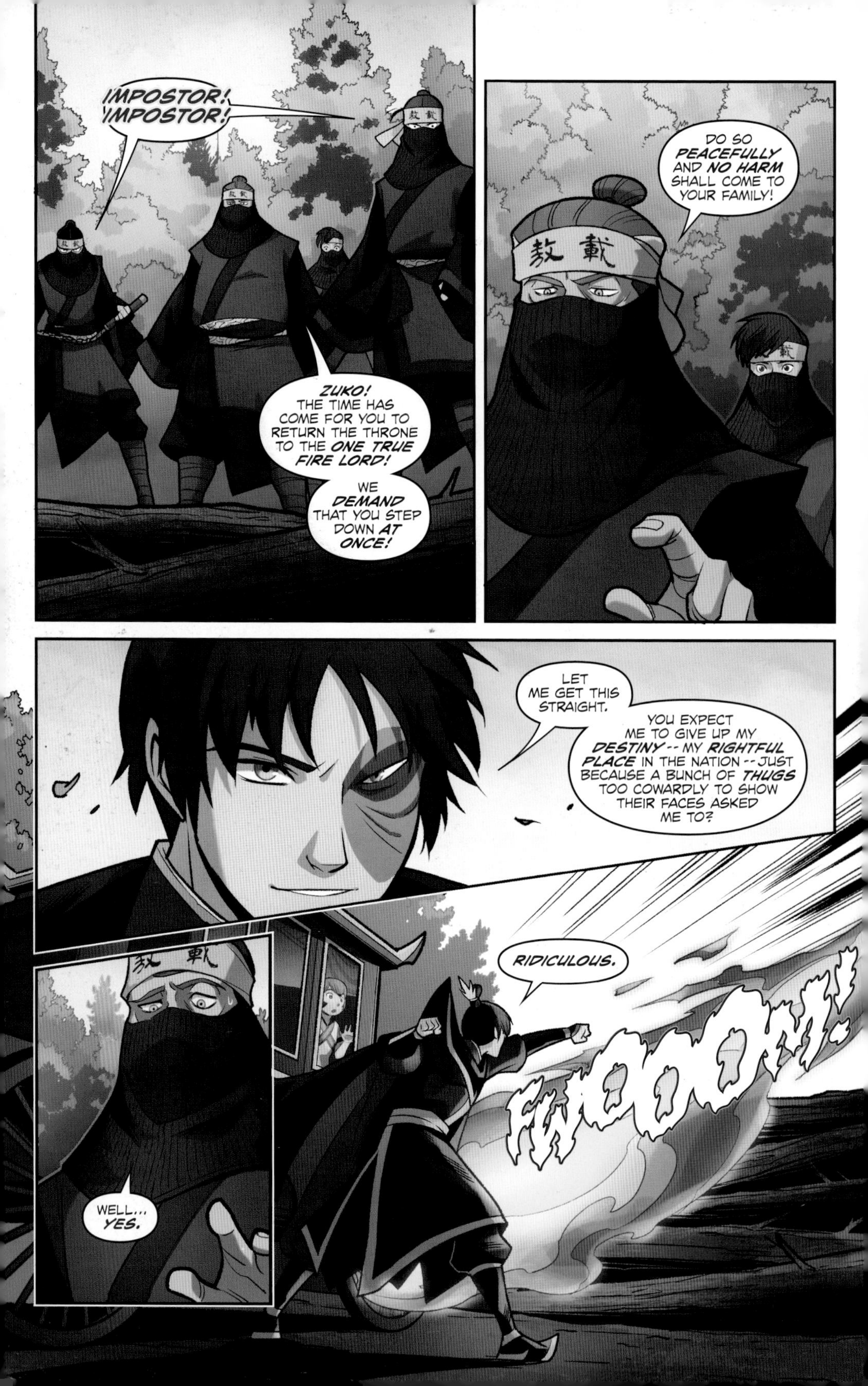
IMPOSTOR! IMPOSTOR!
ZUKO! THE TIME HAS COME FOR YOU TO RETURN THE THRONE TO THE ONE TRUE FIRE LORD!
WE DEMAND THAT YOU STEP DOWN AT ONCE!
DO SO PEACEFULLY AND NO HARM SHALL COME TO YOUR FAMILY!
LET ME GET THIS STRAIGHT.
YOU EXPECT ME TO GIVE UP MY DESTINY -- MY RIGHTFUL PLACE IN THE NATION -- JUST BECAUSE A BUNCH OF THUGS TOO COWARDLY TO SHOW THEIR FACES ASKED ME TO?
WELL... YES.
RIDICULOUS.
FWOOOM!

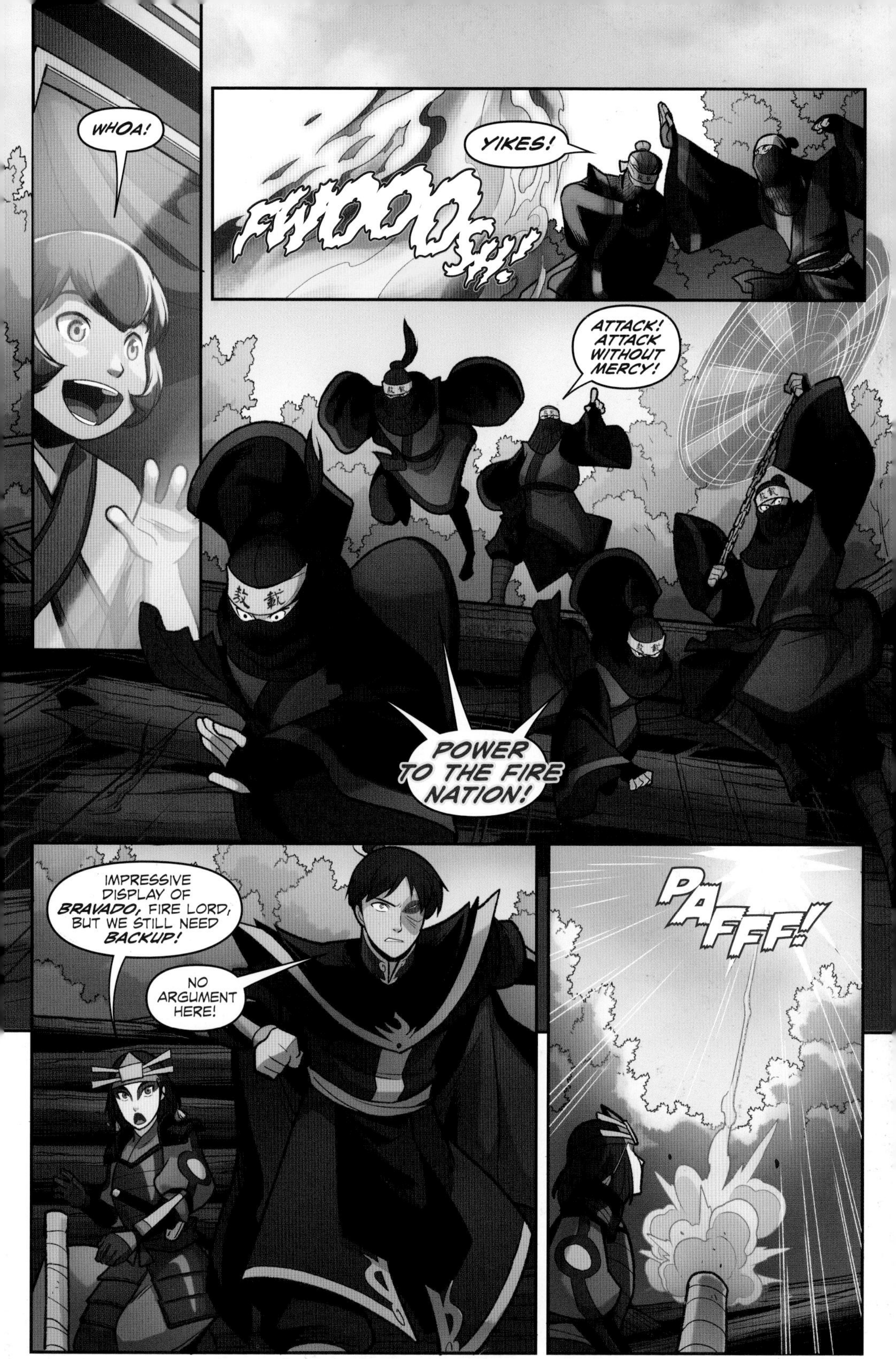
WHOA!
FWOOOSH!
YIKES!
ATTACK! ATTACK WITHOUT MERCY!
POWER TO THE FIRE NATION!
IMPRESSIVE DISPLAY OF BRAVADO, FIRE LORD, BUT WE STILL NEED BACKUP!
NO ARGUMENT HERE!
PAFFF!

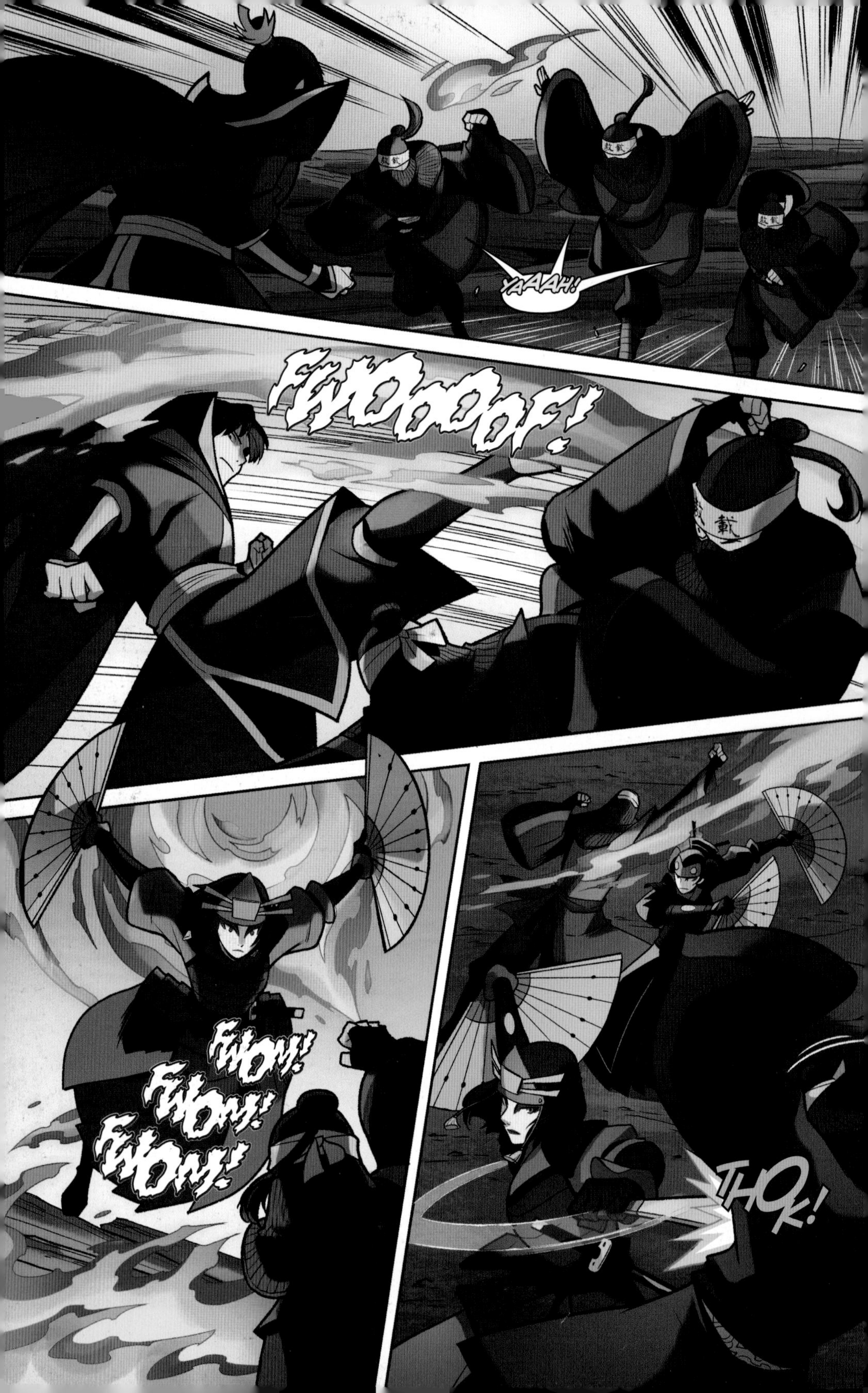
YAAAH!
FWOOOOF!
FWOM!
FWOM!
FWOM!
THOK!

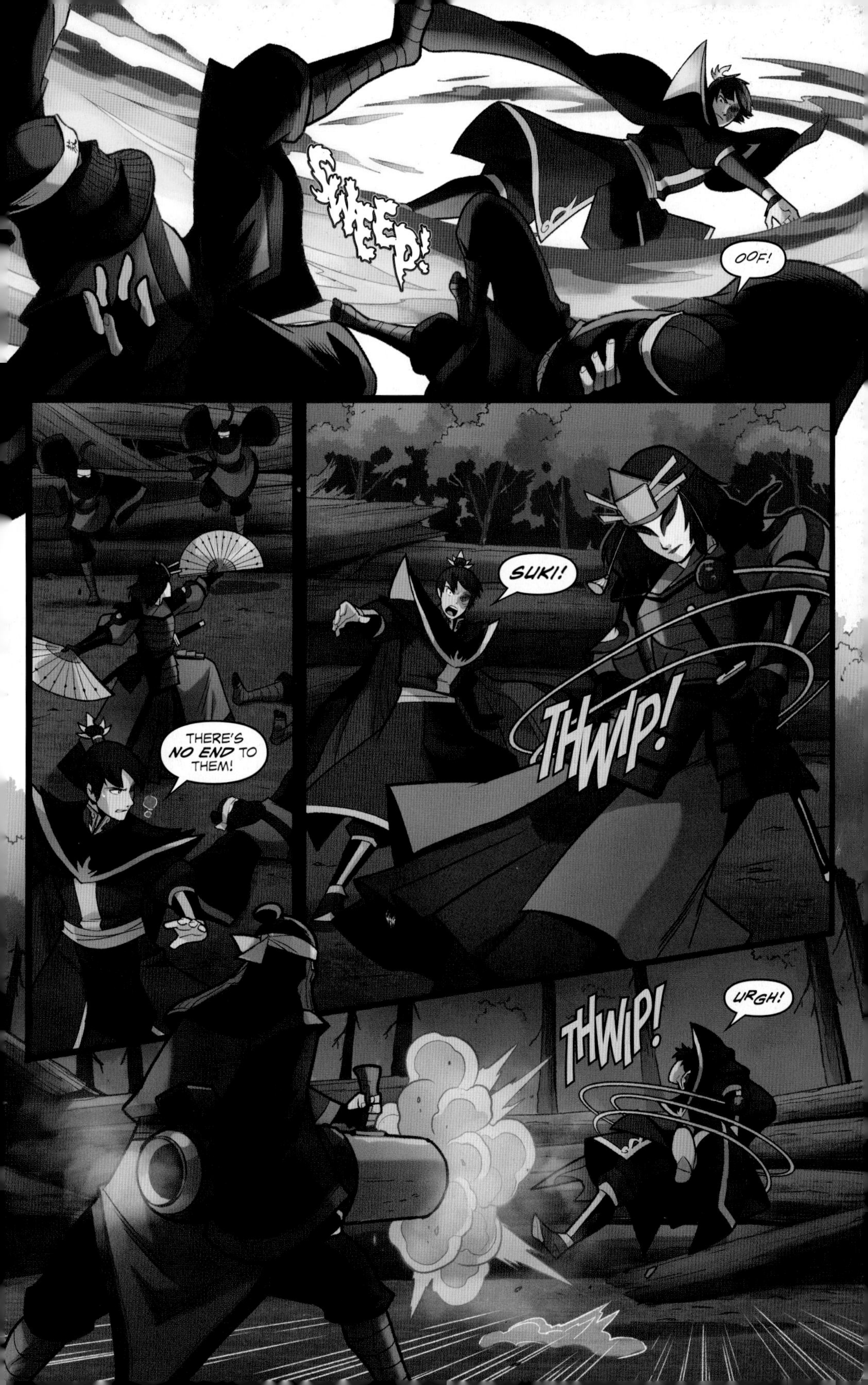
SWEEP!
OOF!
THERE'S NO END TO THEM!
SUKI!
THWIP!
THWIP!
URGH!

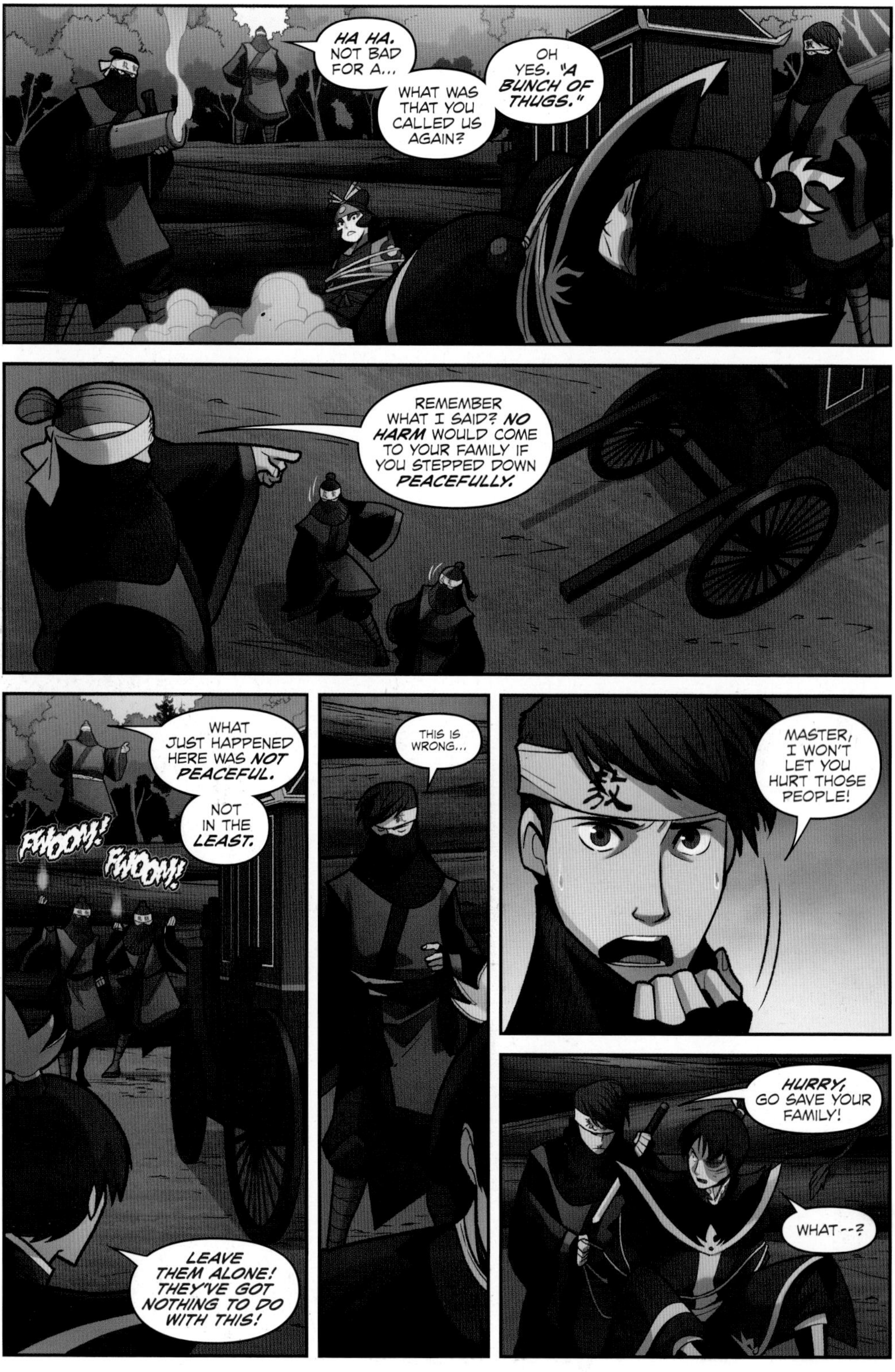
HA HA. NOT BAD FOR A...
WHAT WAS THAT YOU CALLED US AGAIN?
OH YES. "A BUNCH OF THUGS."
REMEMBER WHAT I SAID? NO HARM WOULD COME TO YOUR FAMILY IF YOU STEPPED DOWN PEACEFULLY.
WHAT JUST HAPPENED HERE WAS NOT PEACEFUL.
NOT IN THE LEAST.
FWOOM!
FWOOM!
LEAVE THEM ALONE! THEY'VE GOT NOTHING TO DO WITH THIS!
THIS IS WRONG...
MASTER, I WON'T LET YOU HURT THOSE PEOPLE!
HURRY, GO SAVE YOUR FAMILY!
WHAT--?

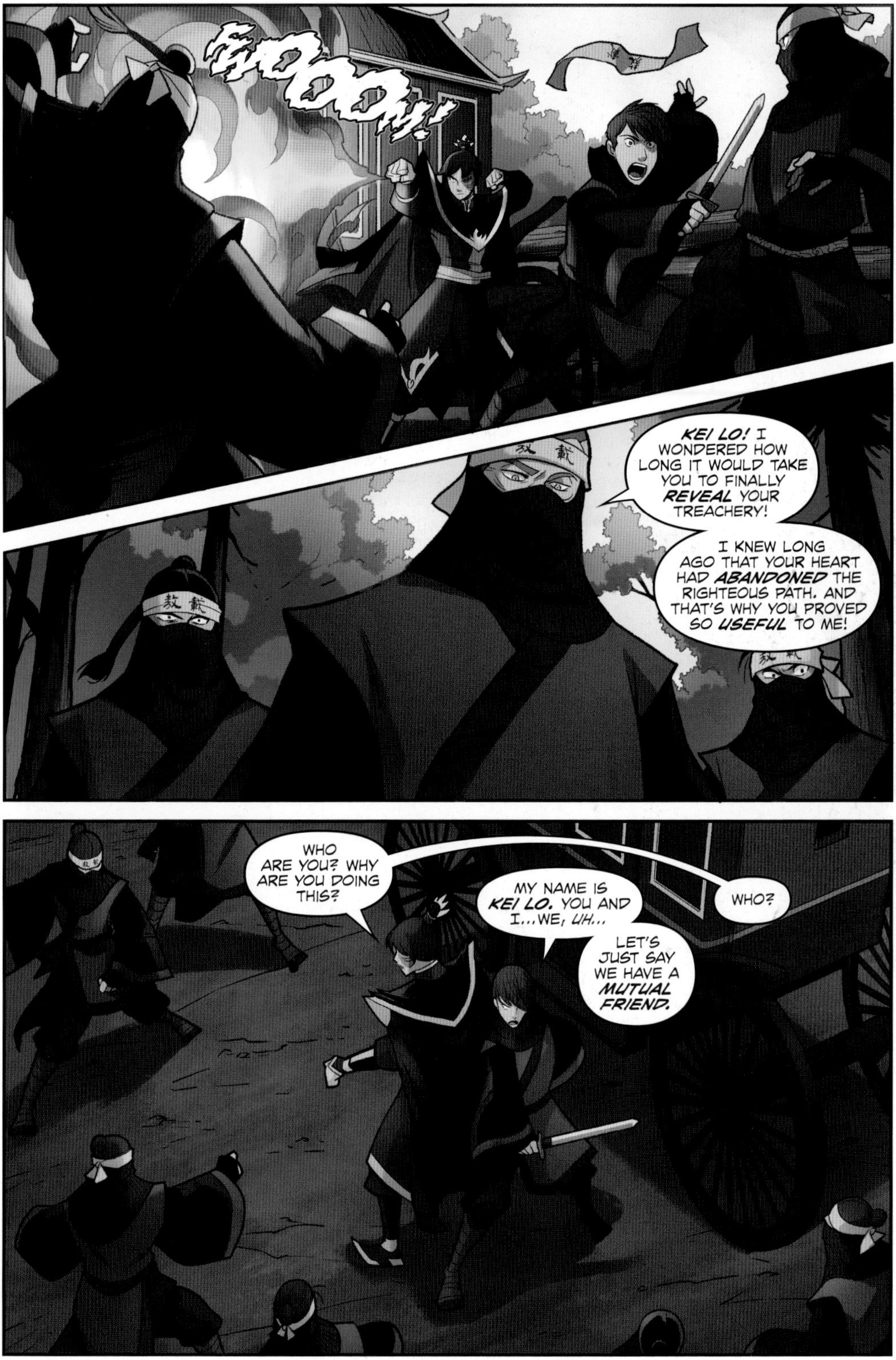
FWOOOM!
KEI LO! I WONDERED HOW LONG IT WOULD TAKE YOU TO FINALLY REVEAL YOUR TREACHERY!
I KNEW LONG AGO THAT YOUR HEART HAD ABANDONED THE RIGHTEOUS PATH. AND THAT'S WHY YOU PROVED SO USEFUL TO ME!
WHO ARE YOU? WHY ARE YOU DOING THIS?
MY NAME IS KEI LO. YOU AND I...WE, UH...
WHO?
LET'S JUST SAY WE HAVE A MUTUAL FRIEND.

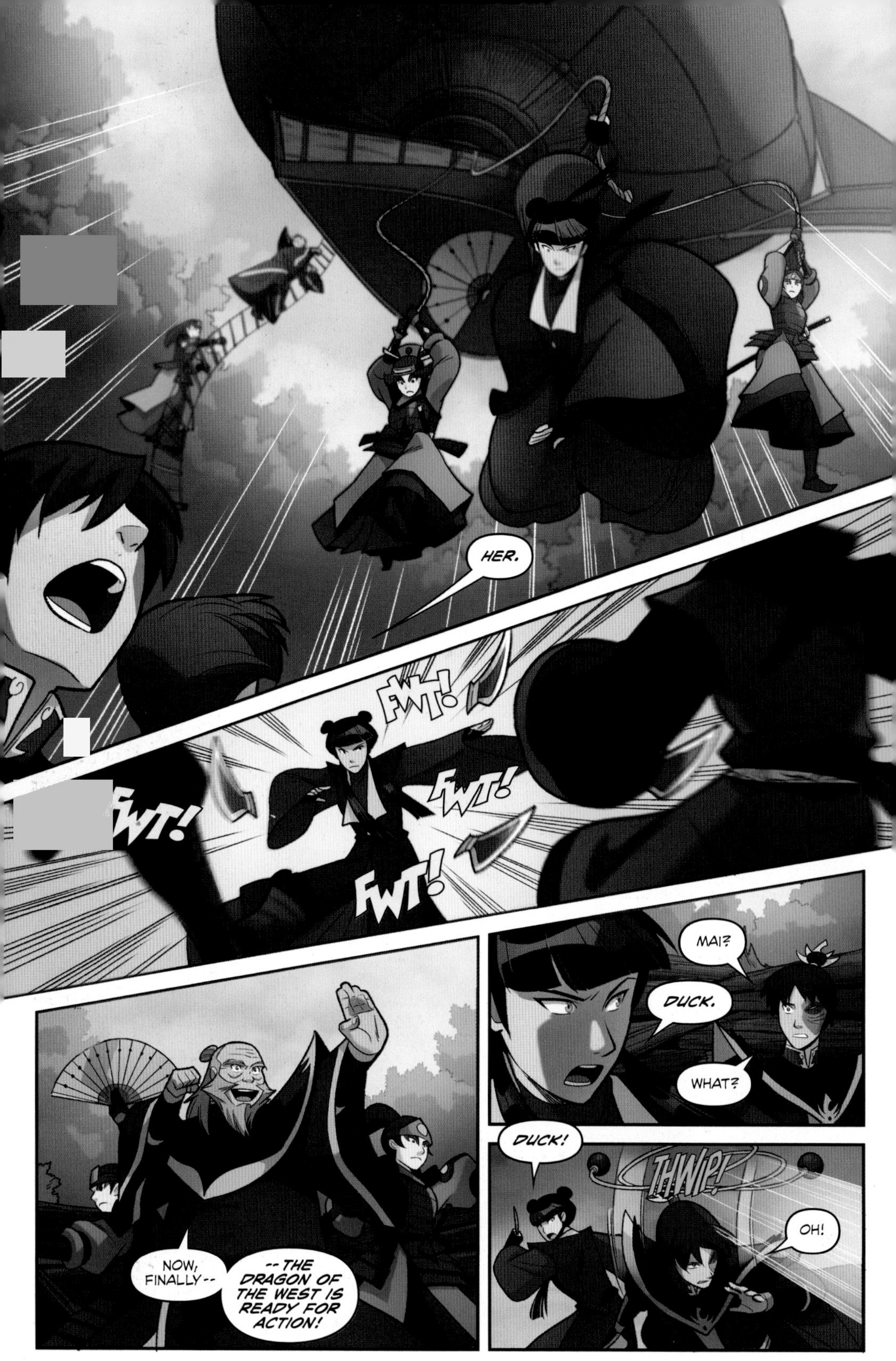
HER.
FWT!
FWT!
FWT!
NOW, FINALLY--
--THE DRAGON OF THE WEST IS READY FOR ACTION!
MAI?
DUCK.
WHAT?
DUCK!
THWIP!
OH!

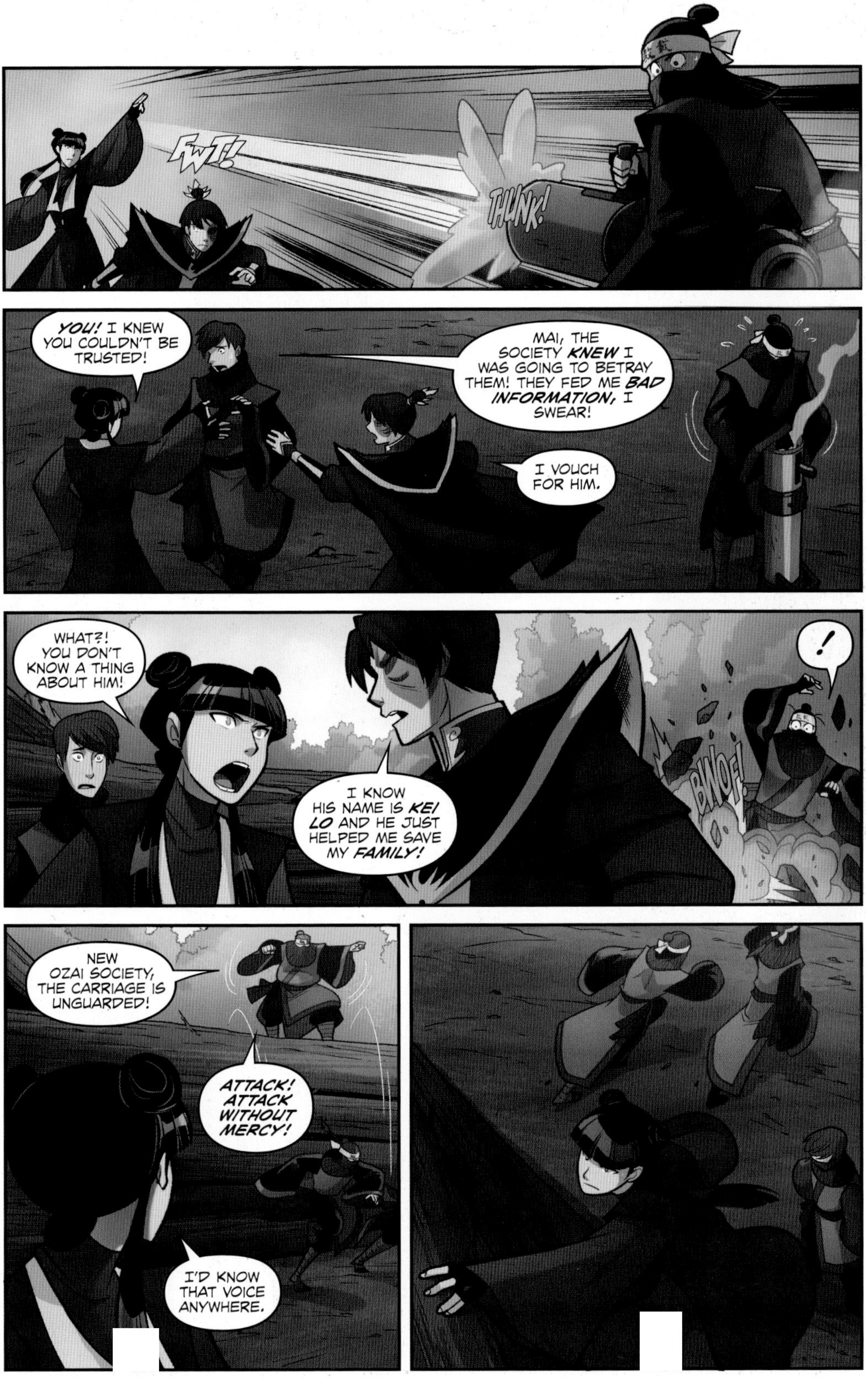
FWT!
THUNK!
YOU! I KNEW YOU COULDN'T BE TRUSTED!
MAI, THE SOCIETY KNEW I WAS GOING TO BETRAY THEM! THEY FED ME BAD INFORMATION, I SWEAR!
I VOUCH FOR HIM.
WHAT?! YOU DON'T KNOW A THING ABOUT HIM!
I KNOW HIS NAME IS KEI LO AND HE JUST HELPED ME SAVE MY FAMILY!
!
BNOF!
NEW OZAI SOCIETY, THE CARRIAGE IS UNGUARDED!
ATTACK! ATTACK WITHOUT MERCY!
I'D KNOW THAT VOICE ANYWHERE.

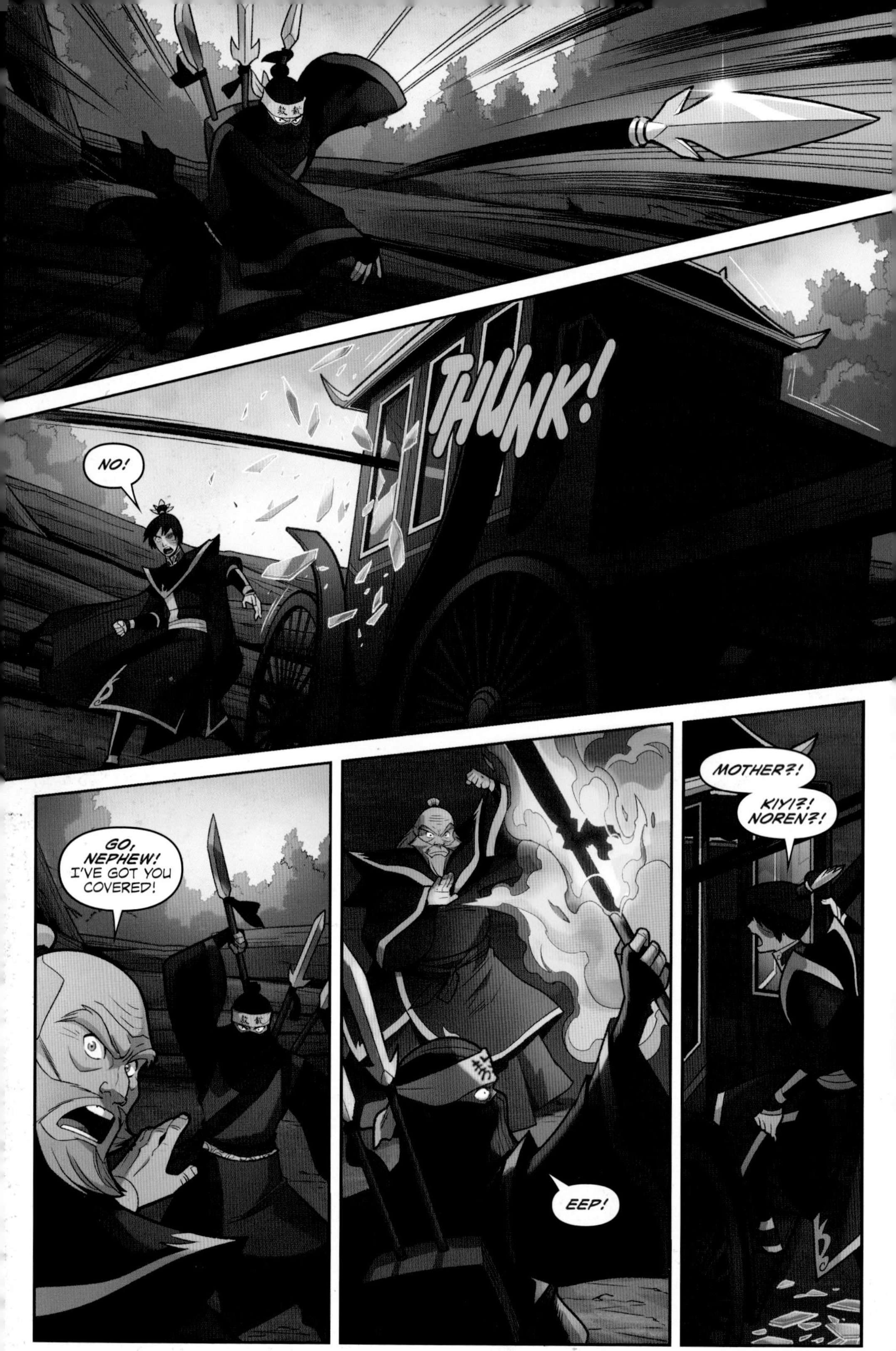
THUNK!
NO!
GO, NEPHEW! I'VE GOT YOU COVERED!
EEP!
MOTHER?!
KIYI?! NOREN?!

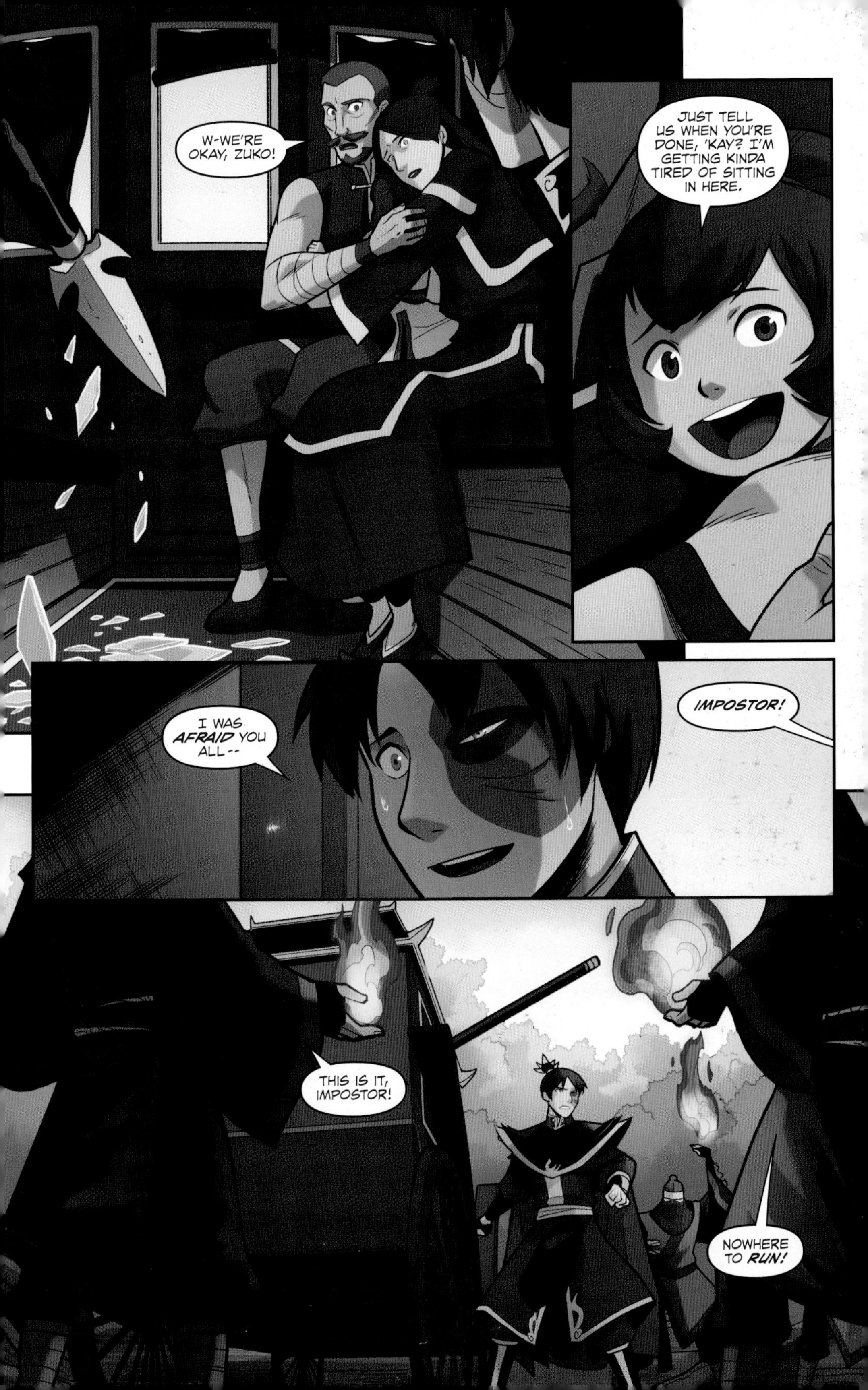
W-WE'RE OKAY, ZUKO!
JUST TELL US WHEN YOU'RE DONE, 'KAY? I'M GETTING KINDA TIRED OF SITTING IN HERE.
I WAS *AFRAID* YOU ALL--
IMPOSTOR!
THIS IS IT, IMPOSTOR!
NOWHERE TO *RUN!*

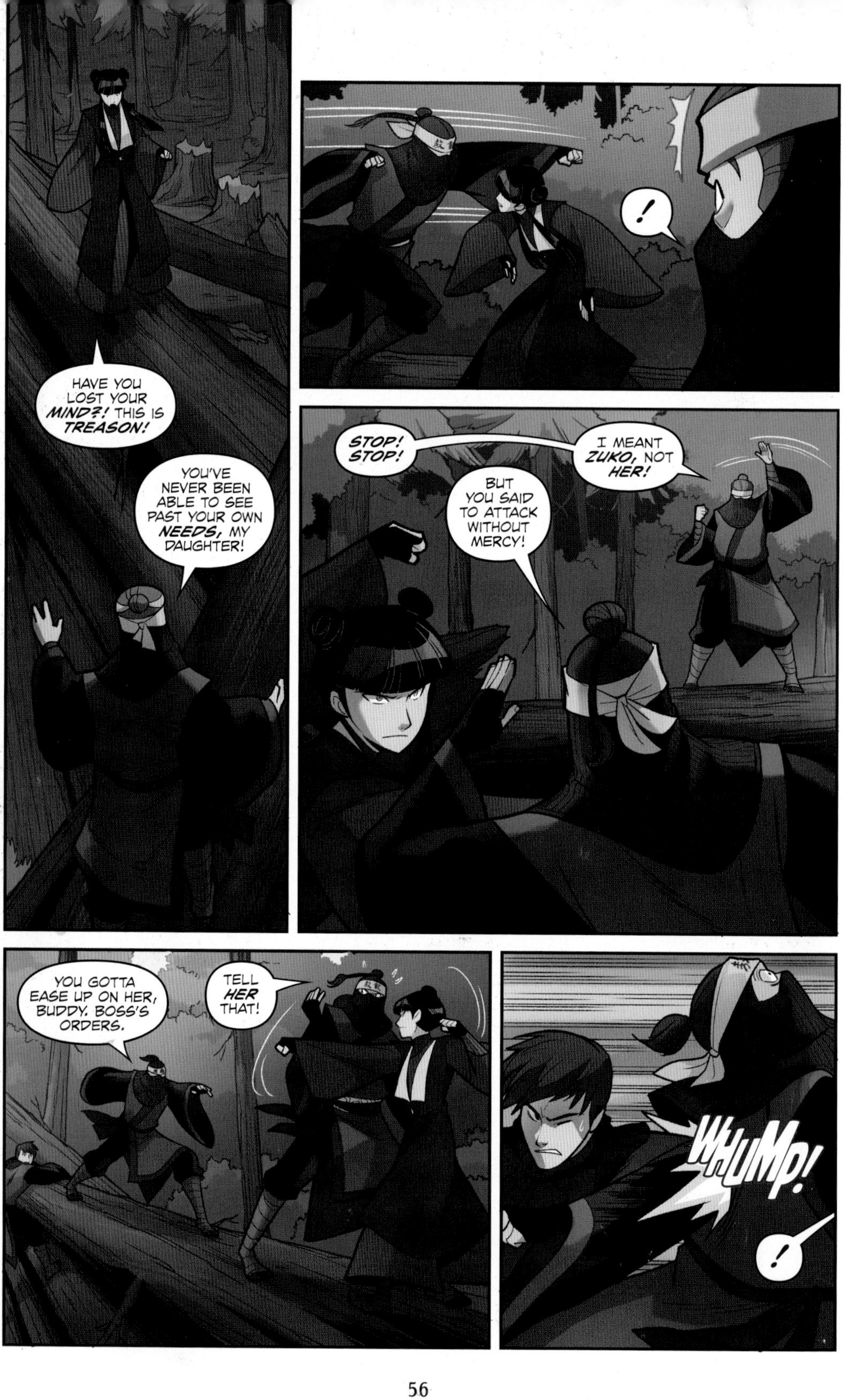
!
HAVE YOU LOST YOUR MIND?! THIS IS TREASON!
YOU'VE NEVER BEEN ABLE TO SEE PAST YOUR OWN NEEDS, MY DAUGHTER!
STOP! STOP!
I MEANT ZUKO, NOT HER!
BUT YOU SAID TO ATTACK WITHOUT MERCY!
YOU GOTTA EASE UP ON HER, BUDDY. BOSS'S ORDERS.
TELL HER THAT!
WHUMP!
!

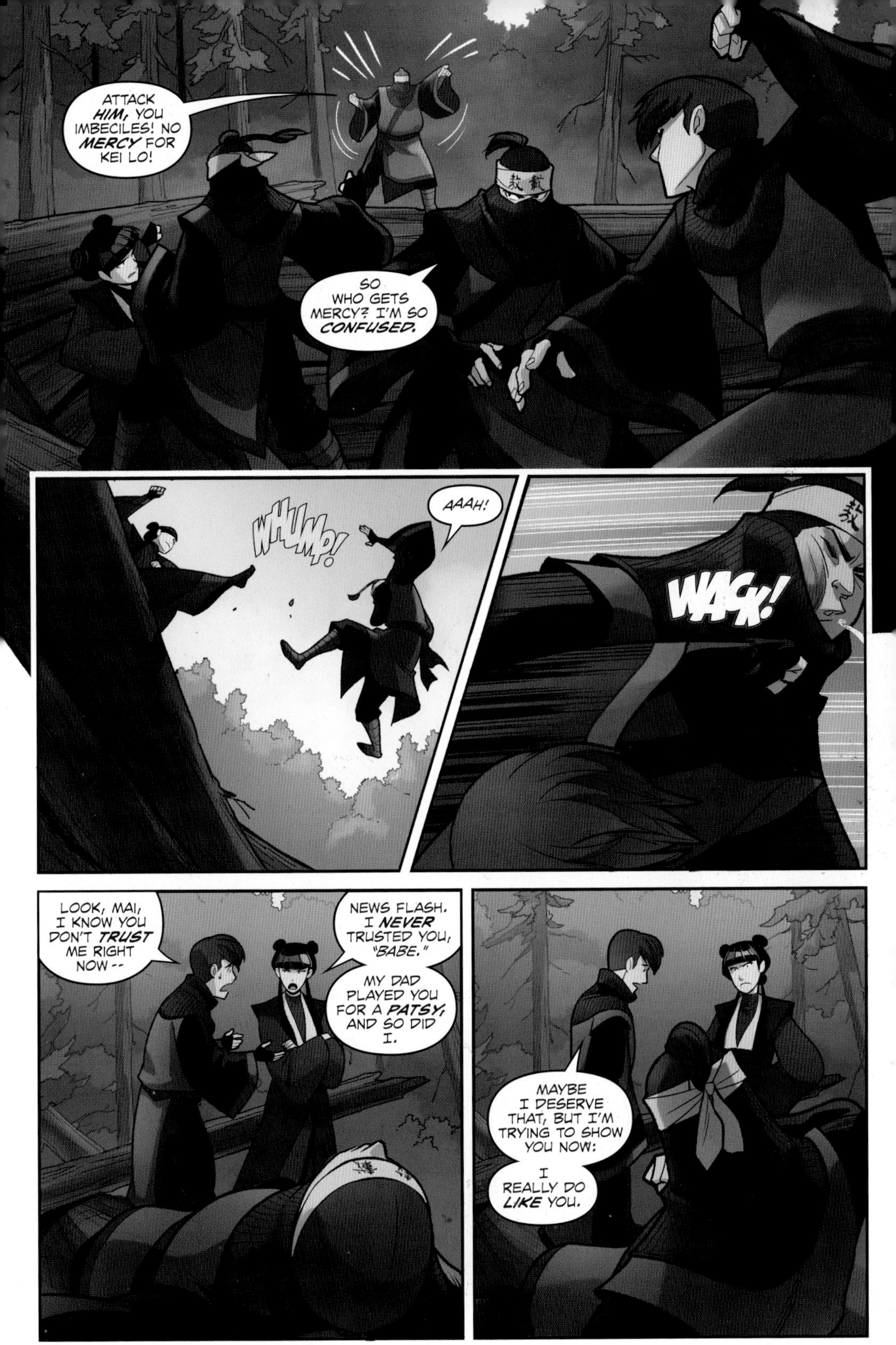
ATTACK HIM, YOU IMBECILES! NO MERCY FOR KEI LO!
SO WHO GETS MERCY? I'M SO CONFUSED.
WHUMP!
AAAH!
WACK!
LOOK, MAI, I KNOW YOU DON'T TRUST ME RIGHT NOW --
NEWS FLASH. I NEVER TRUSTED YOU, "BABE."
MY DAD PLAYED YOU FOR A PATSY, AND SO DID I.
MAYBE I DESERVE THAT, BUT I'M TRYING TO SHOW YOU NOW:
I REALLY DO LIKE YOU.

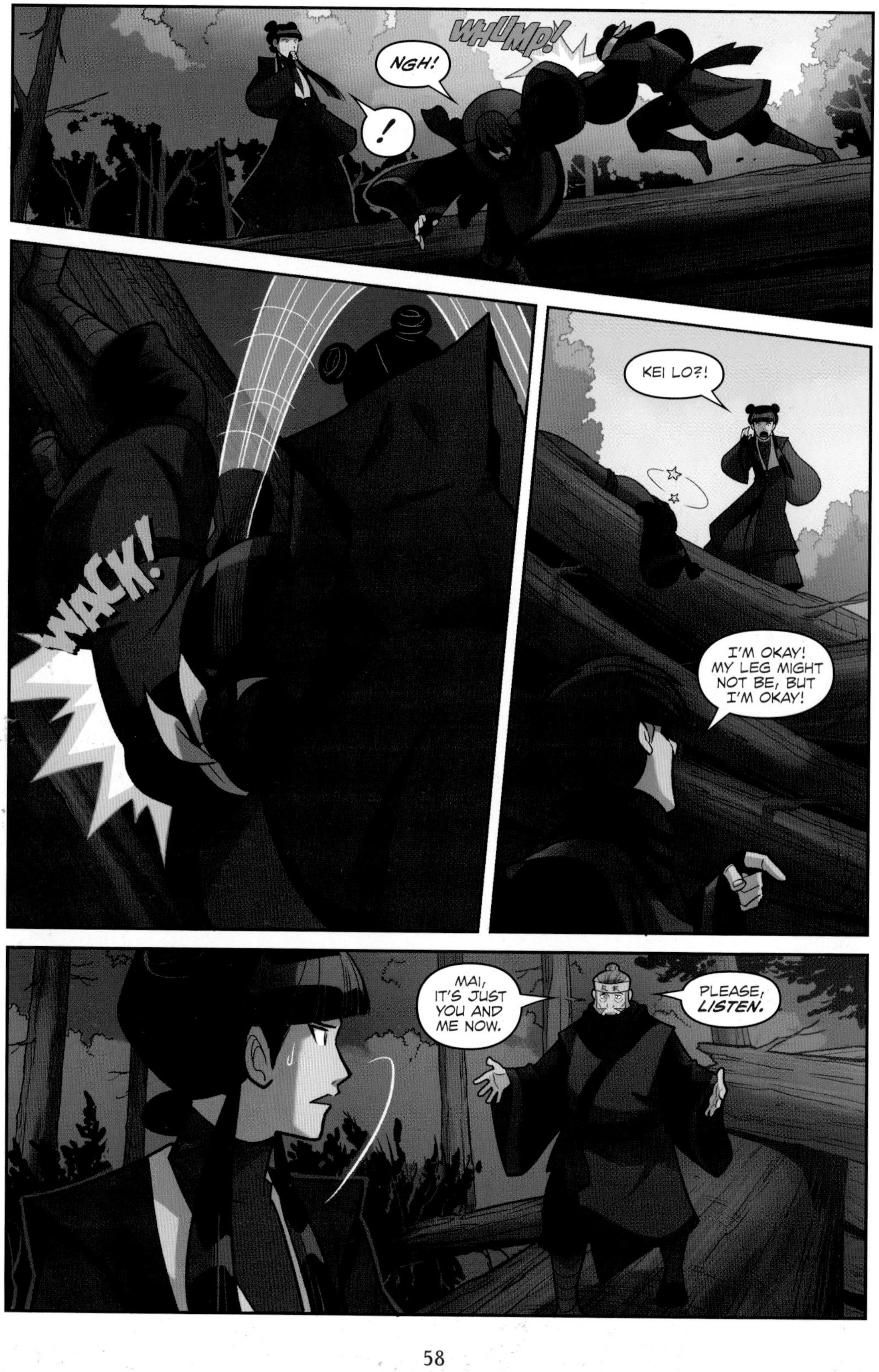
WHUMP!
NGH!
!
WACK!
KEI LO?!
I'M OKAY! MY LEG MIGHT NOT BE, BUT I'M OKAY!
MAI, IT'S JUST YOU AND ME NOW.
PLEASE, LISTEN.

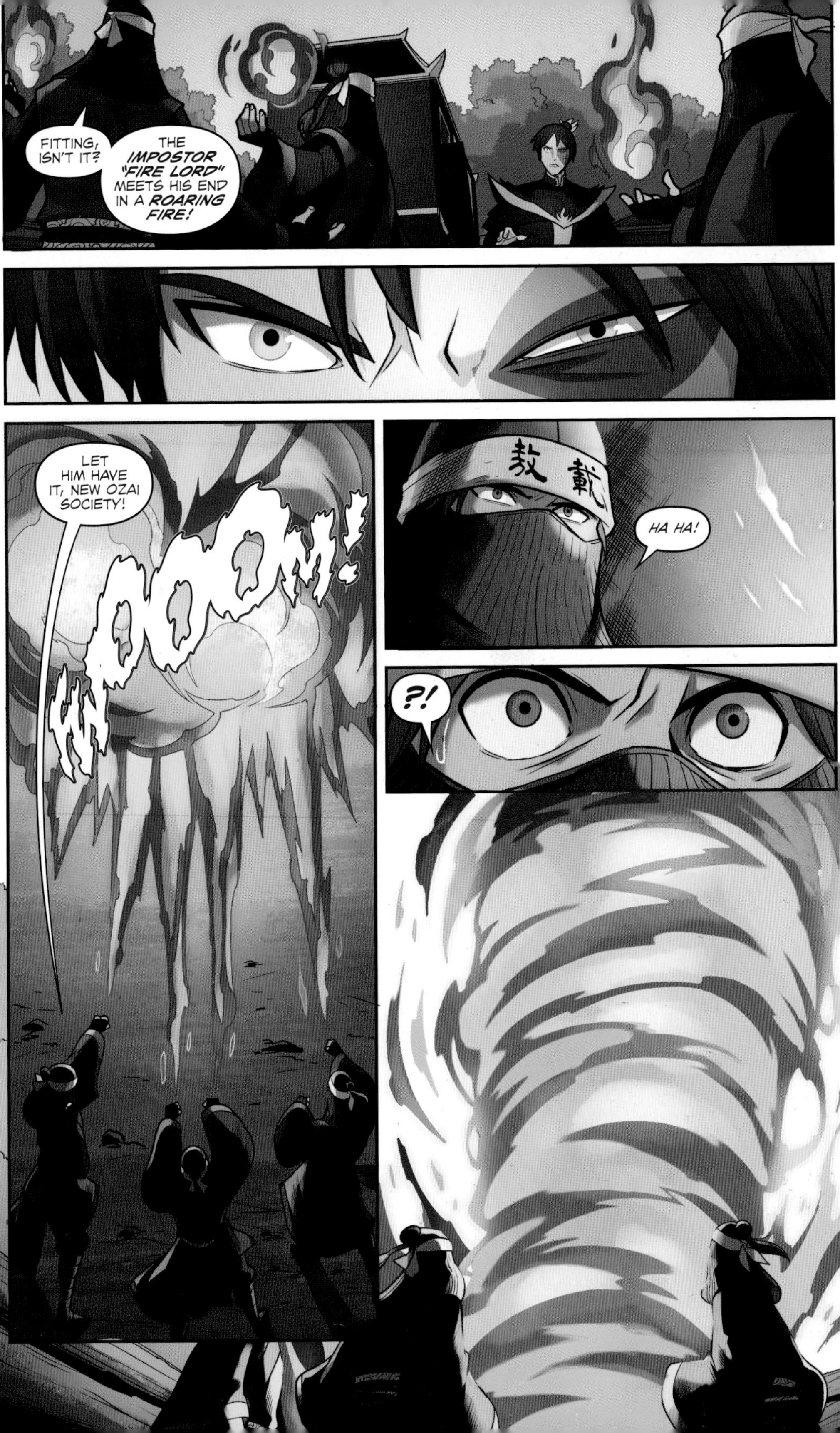
FITTING, ISN'T IT?
THE *IMPOSTOR "FIRE LORD"* MEETS HIS END IN A *ROARING FIRE!*
LET HIM HAVE IT, NEW OZAI SOCIETY!
WHOOOM!
HA HA!
?!

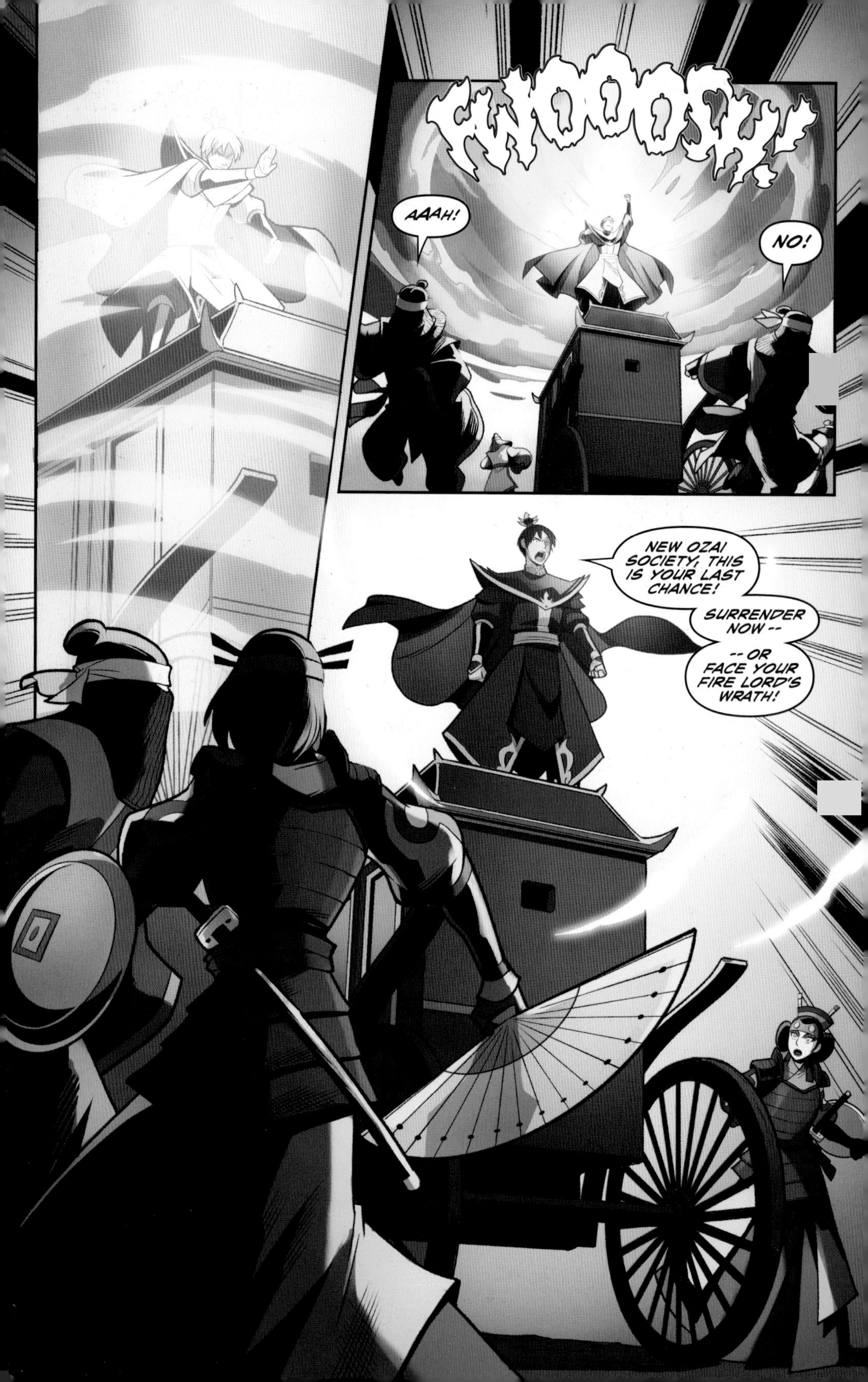
FWOOOSH!
AAAH!
NO!
NEW OZAI SOCIETY, THIS IS YOUR LAST CHANCE!
SURRENDER NOW --
-- OR FACE YOUR FIRE LORD'S WRATH!

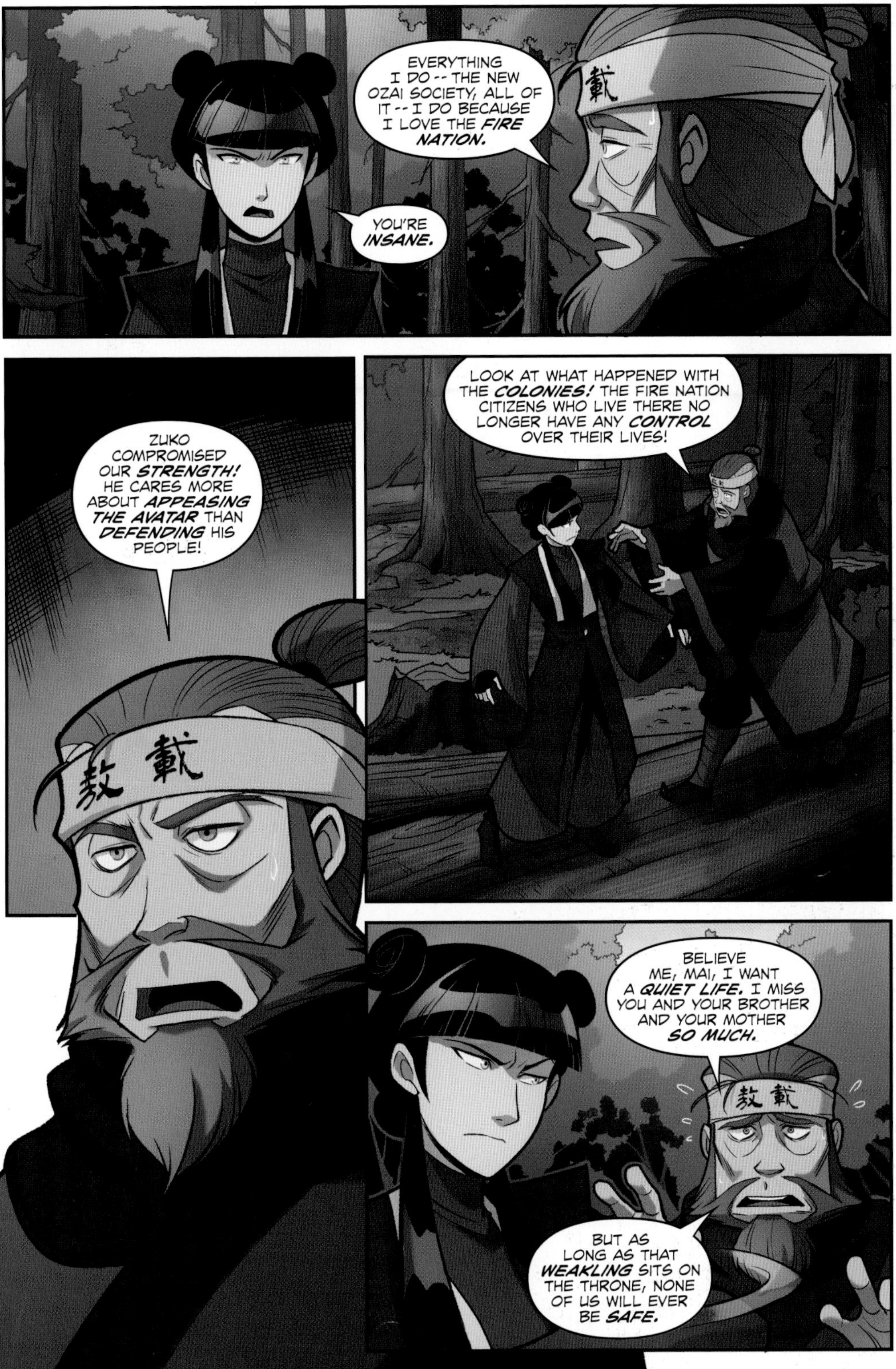
EVERYTHING I DO -- THE NEW OZAI SOCIETY, ALL OF IT -- I DO BECAUSE I LOVE THE FIRE NATION.
YOU'RE INSANE.
ZUKO COMPROMISED OUR STRENGTH! HE CARES MORE ABOUT APPEASING THE AVATAR THAN DEFENDING HIS PEOPLE!
LOOK AT WHAT HAPPENED WITH THE COLONIES! THE FIRE NATION CITIZENS WHO LIVE THERE NO LONGER HAVE ANY CONTROL OVER THEIR LIVES!
BELIEVE ME, MAI, I WANT A QUIET LIFE. I MISS YOU AND YOUR BROTHER AND YOUR MOTHER SO MUCH.
BUT AS LONG AS THAT WEAKLING SITS ON THE THRONE, NONE OF US WILL EVER BE SAFE.

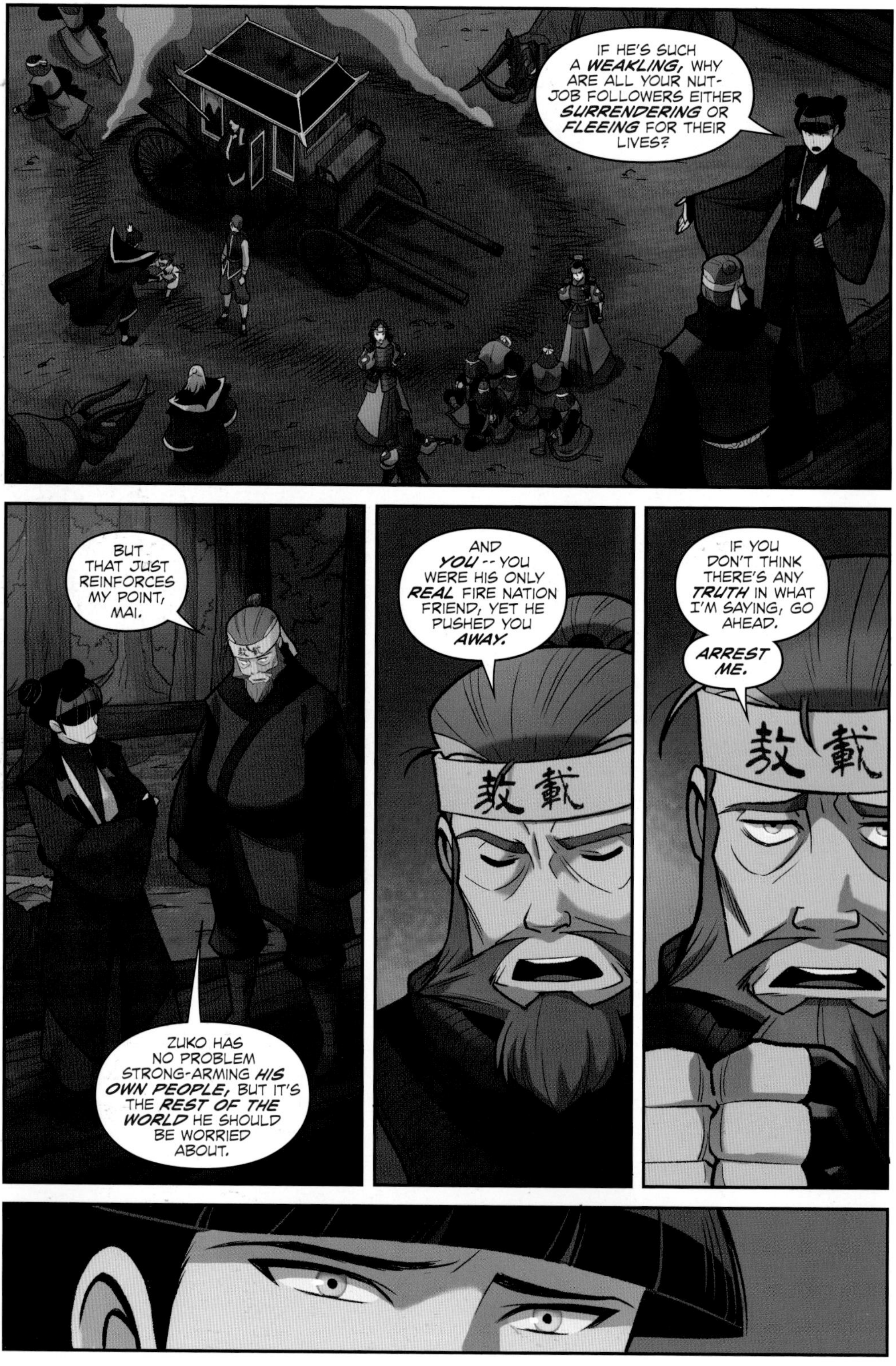
IF HE'S SUCH A WEAKLING, WHY ARE ALL YOUR NUT-JOB FOLLOWERS EITHER SURRENDERING OR FLEEING FOR THEIR LIVES?
BUT THAT JUST REINFORCES MY POINT, MAI.
ZUKO HAS NO PROBLEM STRONG-ARMING HIS OWN PEOPLE, BUT IT'S THE REST OF THE WORLD HE SHOULD BE WORRIED ABOUT.
AND YOU -- YOU WERE HIS ONLY REAL FIRE NATION FRIEND, YET HE PUSHED YOU AWAY.
IF YOU DON'T THINK THERE'S ANY TRUTH IN WHAT I'M SAYING, GO AHEAD.
ARREST ME.

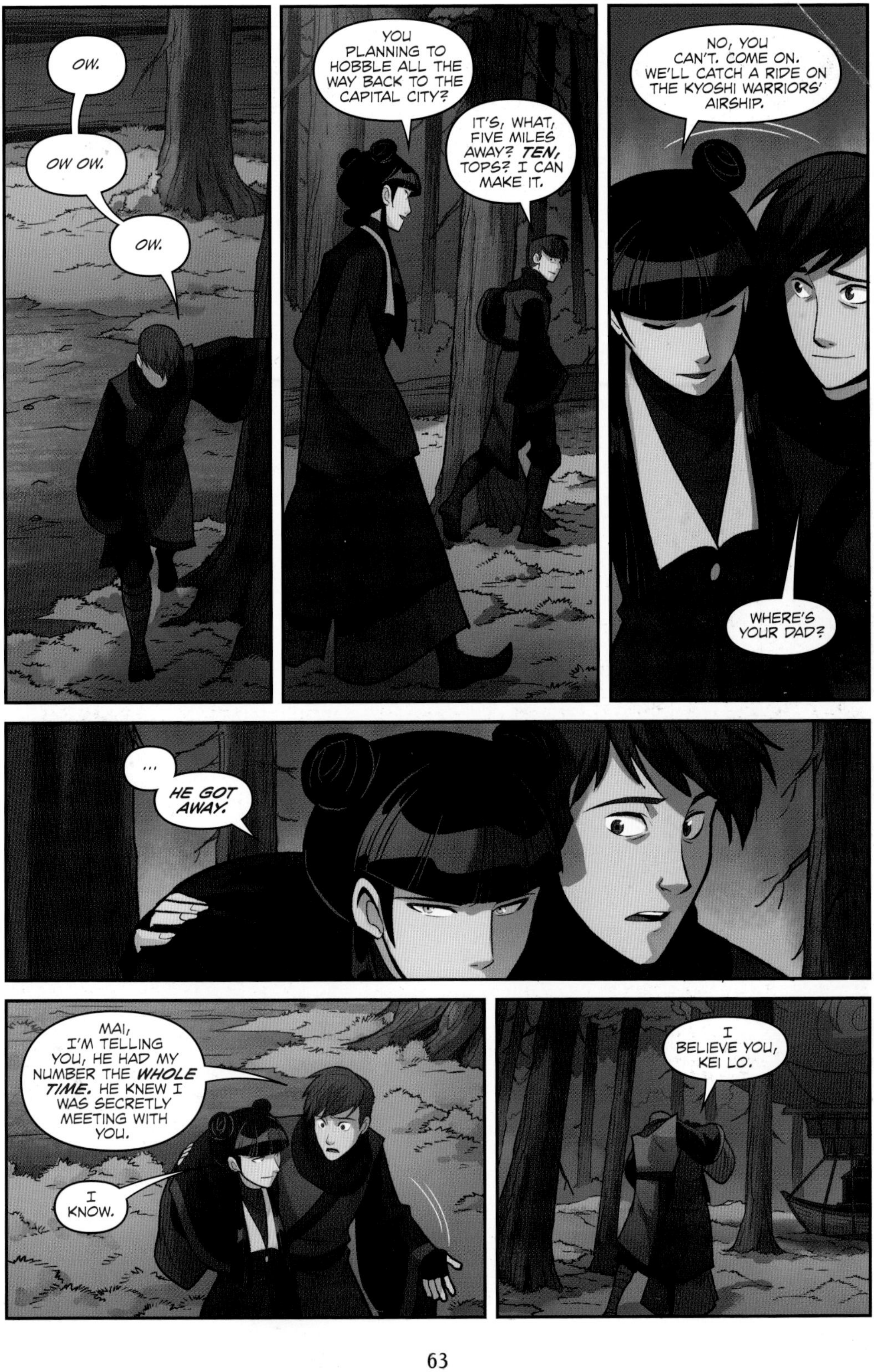
OW.
OW OW.
OW.
YOU PLANNING TO HOBBLE ALL THE WAY BACK TO THE CAPITAL CITY?
IT'S, WHAT, FIVE MILES AWAY? TEN, TOPS? I CAN MAKE IT.
NO, YOU CAN'T. COME ON. WE'LL CATCH A RIDE ON THE KYOSHI WARRIORS' AIRSHIP.
WHERE'S YOUR DAD?
... HE GOT AWAY.
MAI, I'M TELLING YOU, HE HAD MY NUMBER THE WHOLE TIME. HE KNEW I WAS SECRETLY MEETING WITH YOU.
I KNOW.
I BELIEVE YOU, KEI LO.

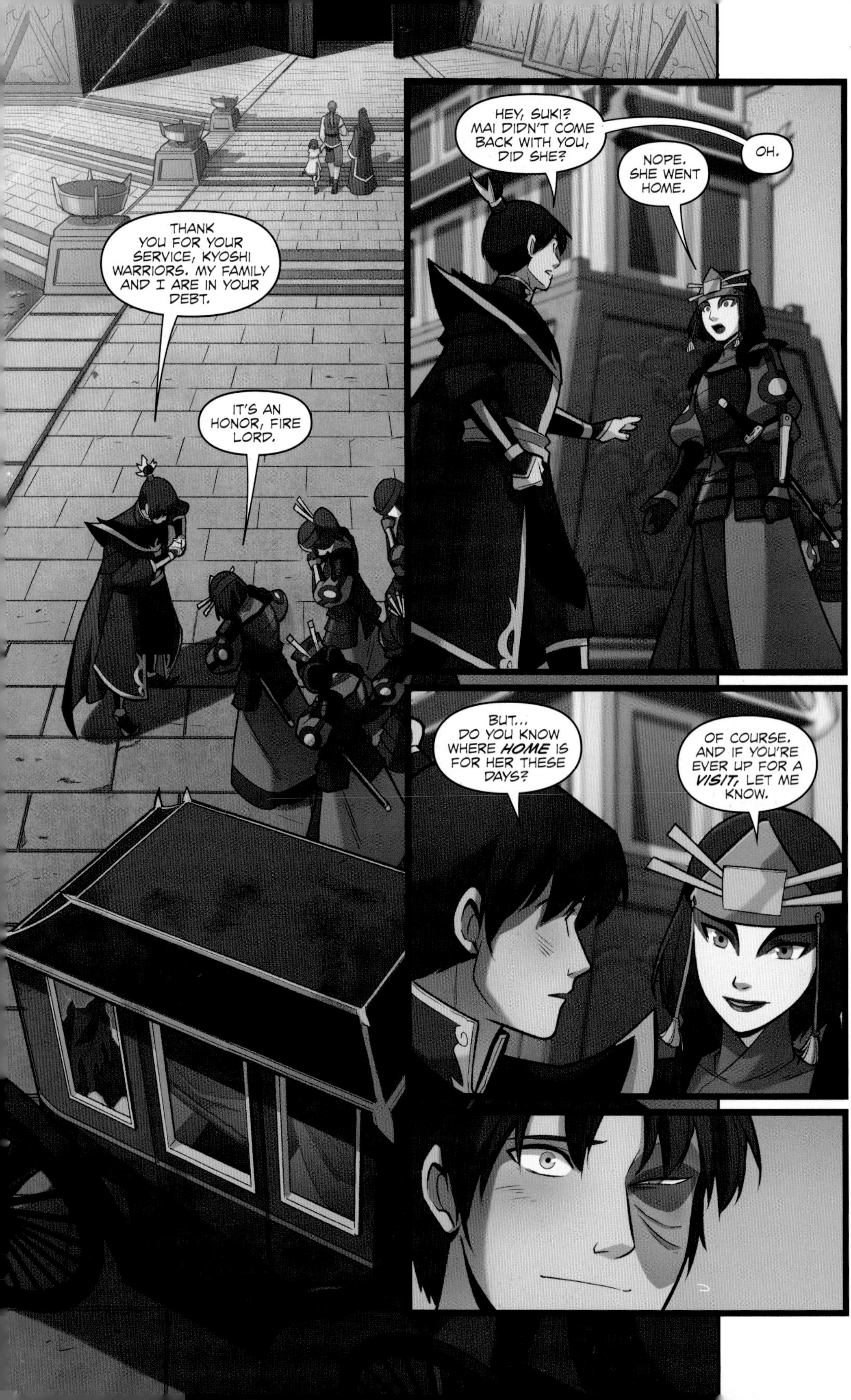
THANK YOU FOR YOUR SERVICE, KYOSHI WARRIORS. MY FAMILY AND I ARE IN YOUR DEBT.
IT'S AN HONOR, FIRE LORD.
HEY, SUKI? MAI DIDN'T COME BACK WITH YOU, DID SHE?
NOPE. SHE WENT HOME.
OH.
BUT... DO YOU KNOW WHERE *HOME* IS FOR HER THESE DAYS?
OF COURSE. AND IF YOU'RE EVER UP FOR A *VISIT,* LET ME KNOW.

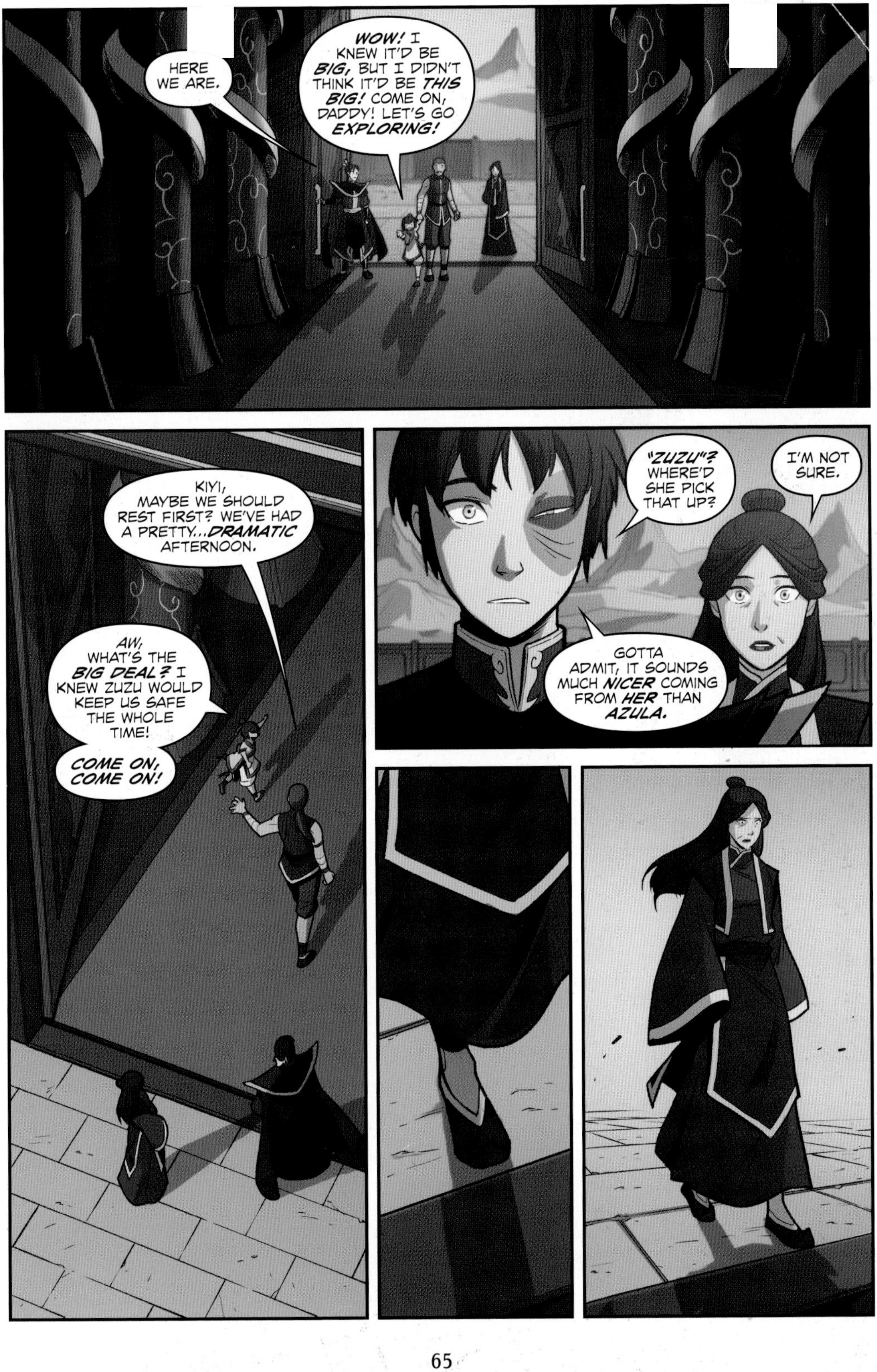
HERE WE ARE.
WOW! I KNEW IT'D BE BIG, BUT I DIDN'T THINK IT'D BE THIS BIG! COME ON, DADDY! LET'S GO EXPLORING!
KIYI, MAYBE WE SHOULD REST FIRST? WE'VE HAD A PRETTY...DRAMATIC AFTERNOON.
AW, WHAT'S THE BIG DEAL? I KNEW ZUZU WOULD KEEP US SAFE THE WHOLE TIME!
COME ON, COME ON!
"ZUZU"? WHERE'D SHE PICK THAT UP?
I'M NOT SURE.
GOTTA ADMIT, IT SOUNDS MUCH NICER COMING FROM HER THAN AZULA.

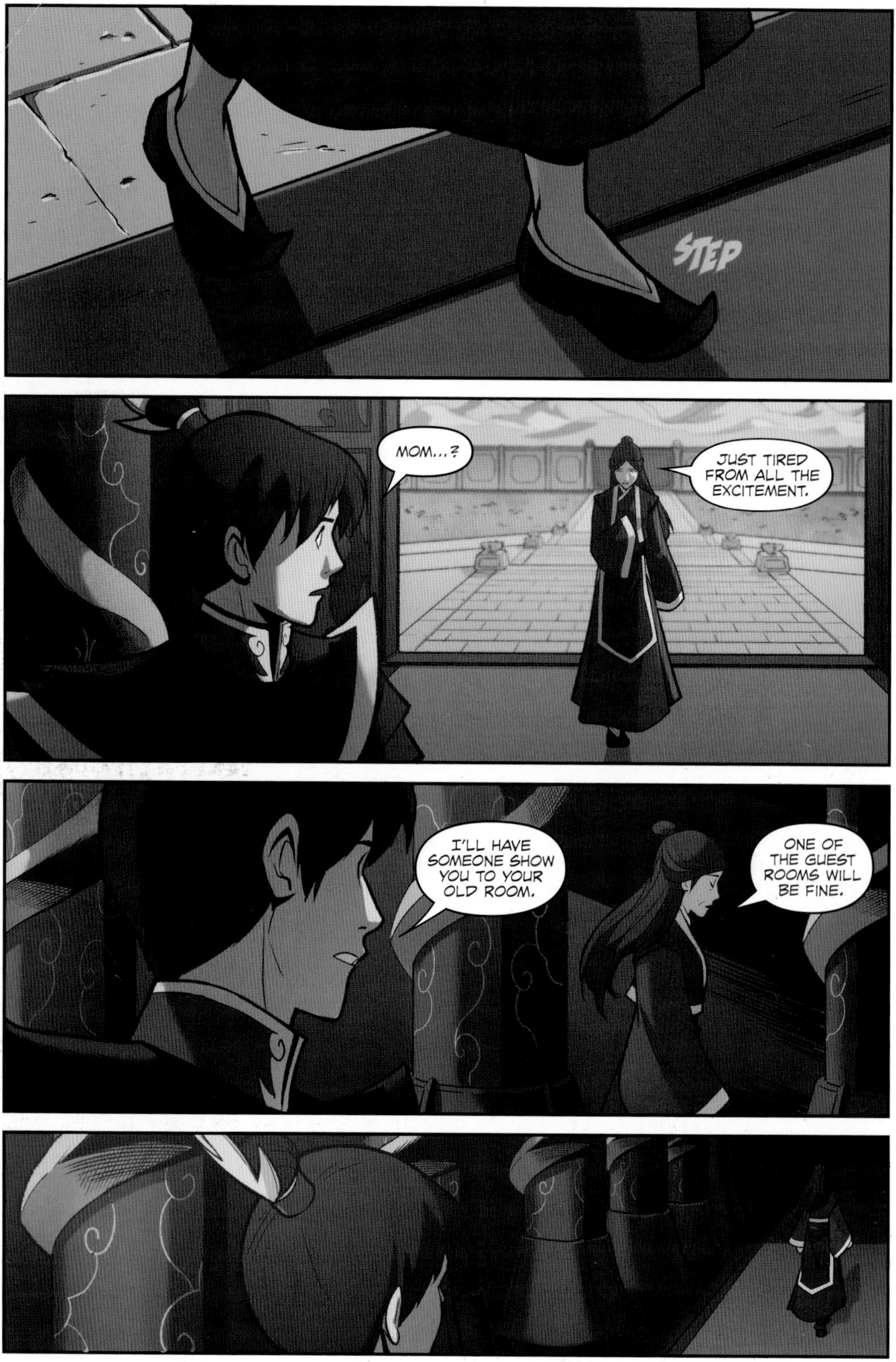

STEP
MOM...?
JUST TIRED FROM ALL THE EXCITEMENT.
I'LL HAVE SOMEONE SHOW YOU TO YOUR OLD ROOM.
ONE OF THE GUEST ROOMS WILL BE FINE.

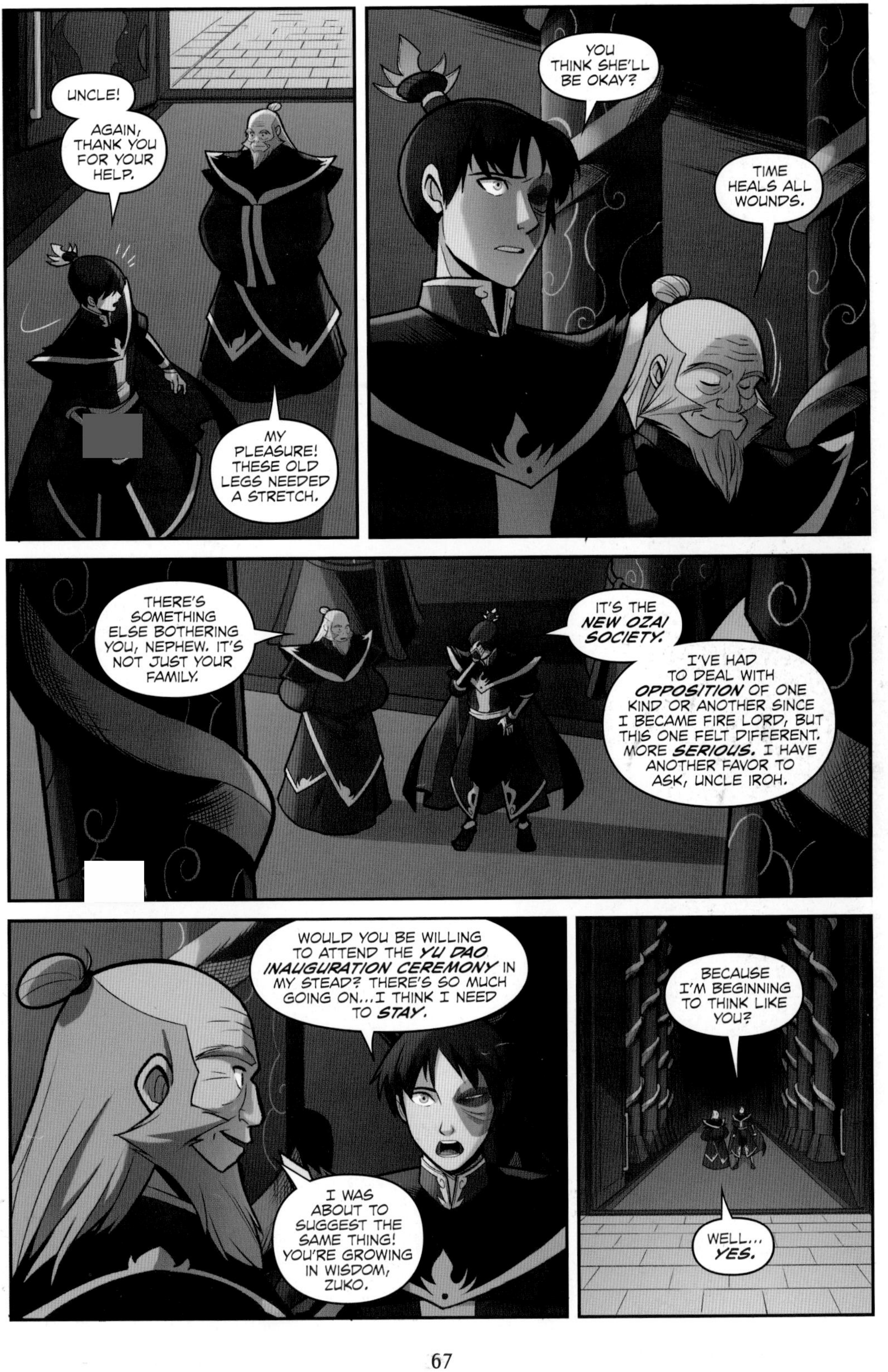
UNCLE!
AGAIN, THANK YOU FOR YOUR HELP.
MY PLEASURE! THESE OLD LEGS NEEDED A STRETCH.
YOU THINK SHE'LL BE OKAY?
TIME HEALS ALL WOUNDS.
THERE'S SOMETHING ELSE BOTHERING YOU, NEPHEW. IT'S NOT JUST YOUR FAMILY.
IT'S THE *NEW OZAI SOCIETY.*
I'VE HAD TO DEAL WITH *OPPOSITION* OF ONE KIND OR ANOTHER SINCE I BECAME FIRE LORD, BUT THIS ONE FELT DIFFERENT. MORE *SERIOUS.* I HAVE ANOTHER FAVOR TO ASK, UNCLE IROH.
WOULD YOU BE WILLING TO ATTEND THE *YU DAO INAUGURATION CEREMONY* IN MY STEAD? THERE'S SO MUCH GOING ON...I THINK I NEED TO *STAY.*
I WAS ABOUT TO SUGGEST THE SAME THING! YOU'RE GROWING IN WISDOM, ZUKO.
BECAUSE I'M BEGINNING TO THINK LIKE YOU?
WELL... *YES.*

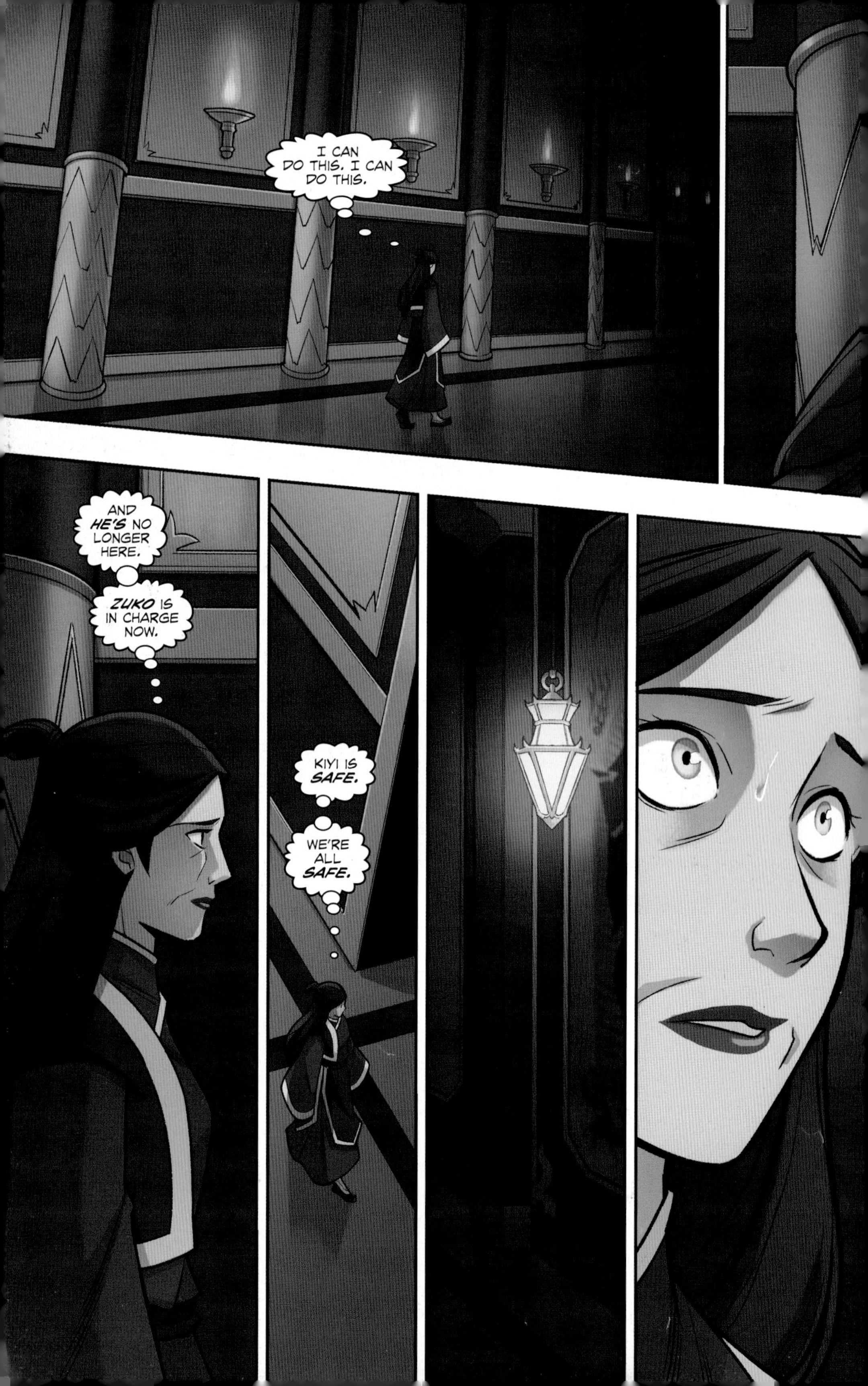
I CAN DO THIS. I CAN DO THIS.
AND HE'S NO LONGER HERE.
ZUKO IS IN CHARGE NOW.
KIYI IS SAFE.
WE'RE ALL SAFE.

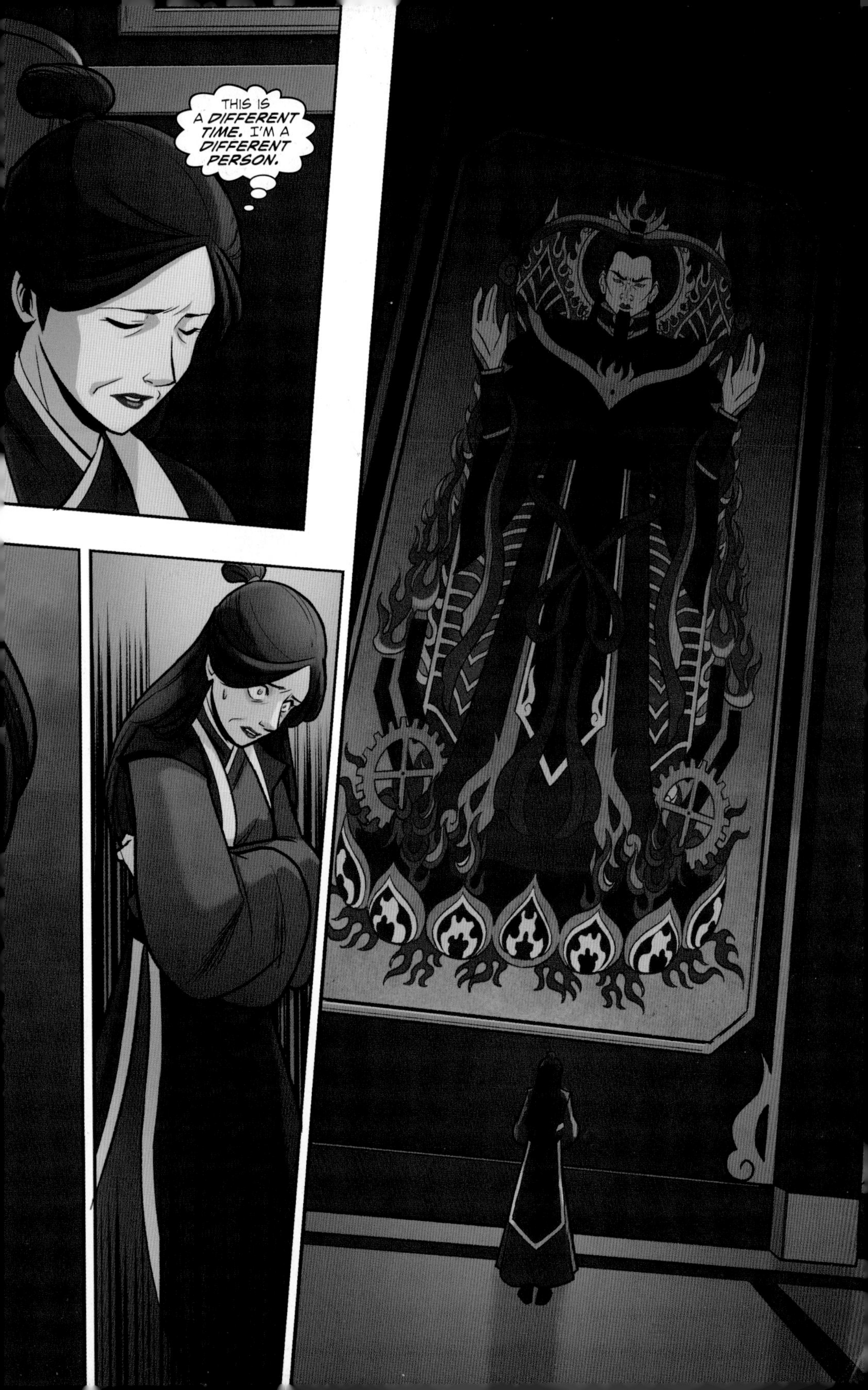
THIS IS A *DIFFERENT TIME.* I'M A *DIFFERENT PERSON.*

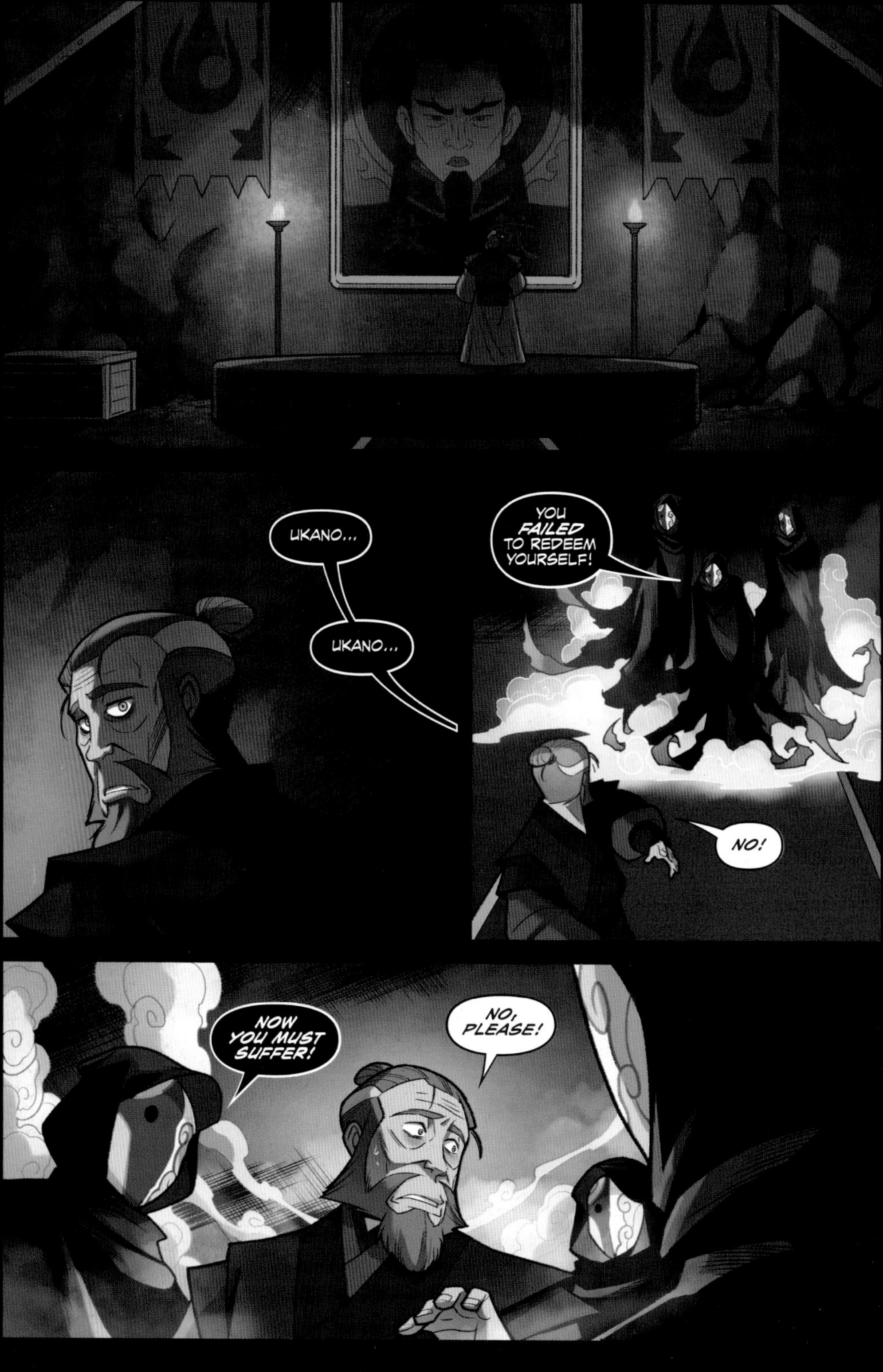
UKANO...
UKANO...
YOU FAILED TO REDEEM YOURSELF!
NO!
NOW YOU MUST SUFFER!
NO, PLEASE!

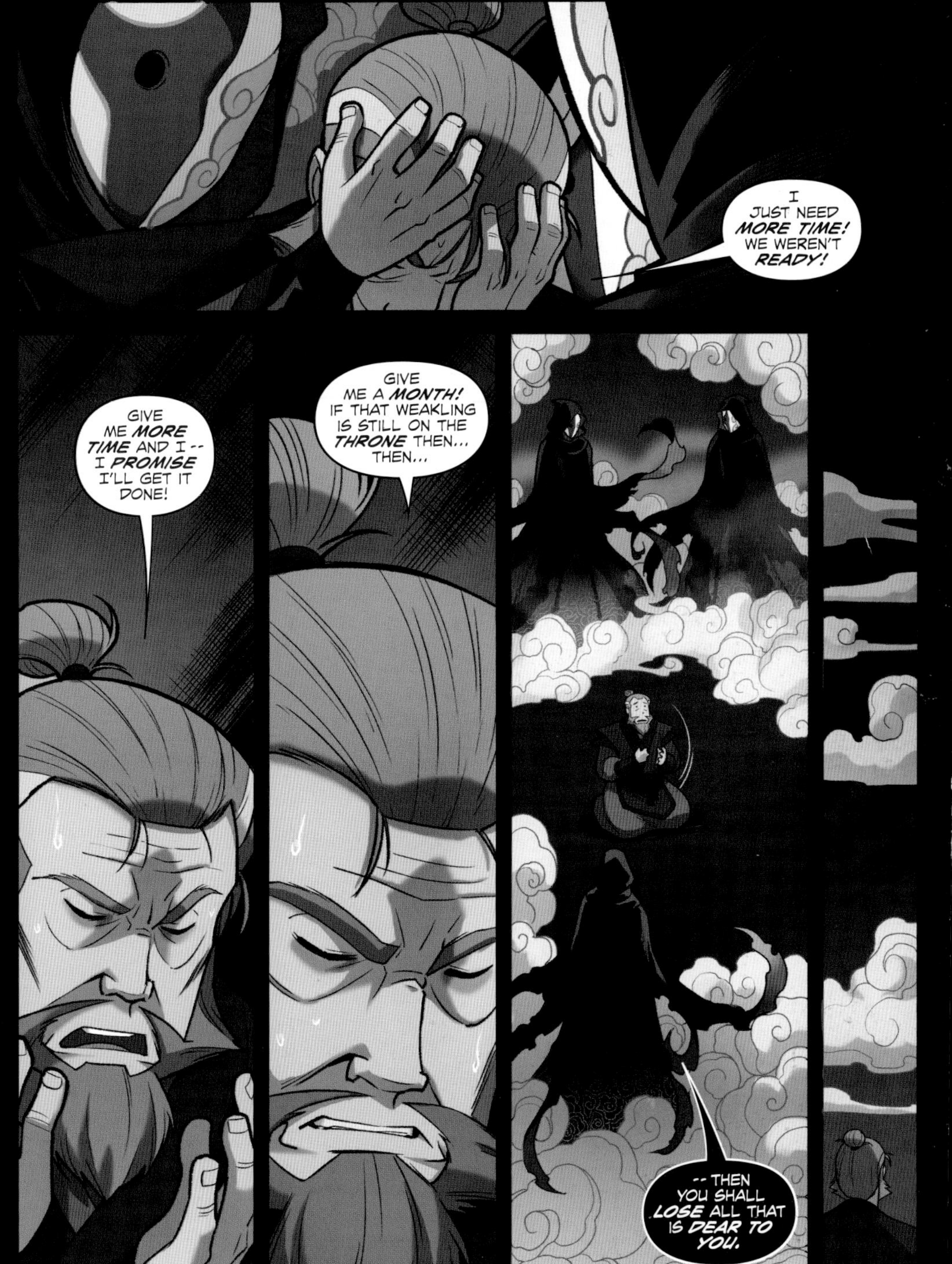
I JUST NEED MORE TIME! WE WEREN'T READY!
GIVE ME MORE TIME AND I -- I PROMISE I'LL GET IT DONE!
GIVE ME A MONTH! IF THAT WEAKLING IS STILL ON THE THRONE THEN... THEN...
-- THEN YOU SHALL LOSE ALL THAT IS DEAR TO YOU.

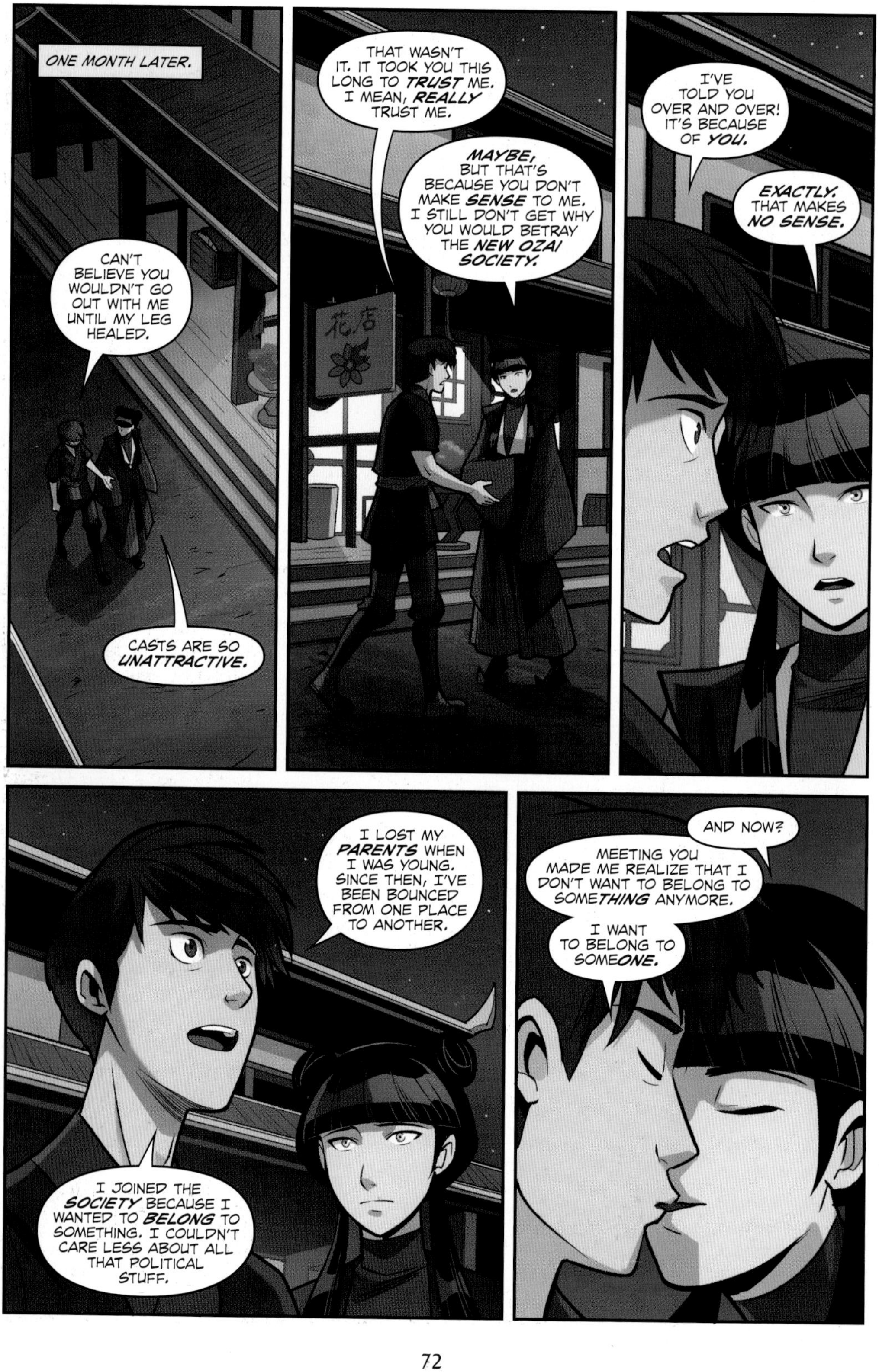
ONE MONTH LATER.
CAN'T BELIEVE YOU WOULDN'T GO OUT WITH ME UNTIL MY LEG HEALED.
CASTS ARE SO UNATTRACTIVE.
THAT WASN'T IT. IT TOOK YOU THIS LONG TO TRUST ME. I MEAN, REALLY TRUST ME.
MAYBE, BUT THAT'S BECAUSE YOU DON'T MAKE SENSE TO ME. I STILL DON'T GET WHY YOU WOULD BETRAY THE NEW OZAI SOCIETY.
花店
I'VE TOLD YOU OVER AND OVER! IT'S BECAUSE OF YOU.
EXACTLY. THAT MAKES NO SENSE.
I LOST MY PARENTS WHEN I WAS YOUNG. SINCE THEN, I'VE BEEN BOUNCED FROM ONE PLACE TO ANOTHER.
I JOINED THE SOCIETY BECAUSE I WANTED TO BELONG TO SOMETHING. I COULDN'T CARE LESS ABOUT ALL THAT POLITICAL STUFF.
AND NOW?
MEETING YOU MADE ME REALIZE THAT I DON'T WANT TO BELONG TO SOMETHING ANYMORE.
I WANT TO BELONG TO SOMEONE.

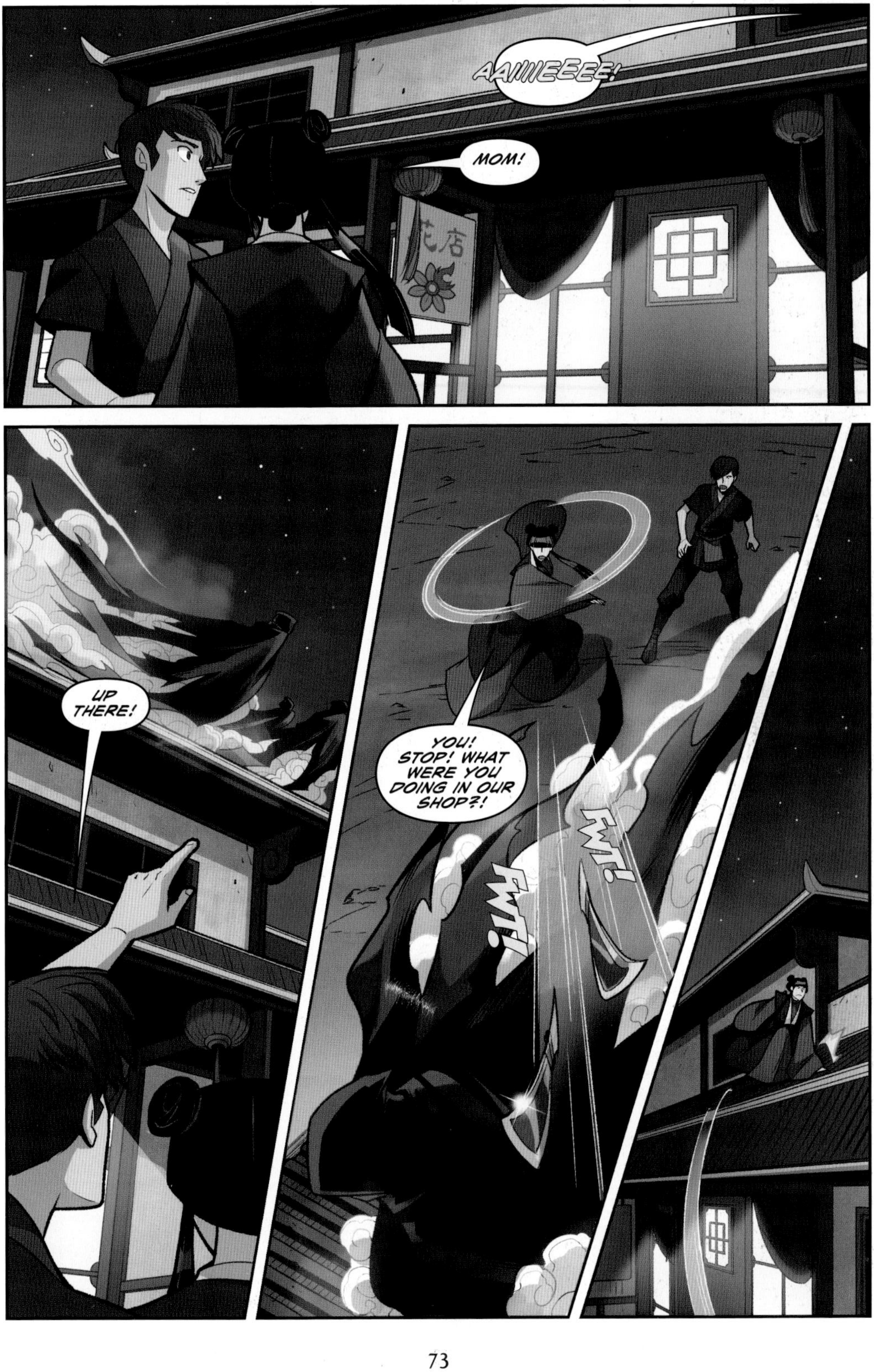
AAIIIIEEEEE!
MOM!
花店
UP THERE!
YOU! STOP! WHAT WERE YOU DOING IN OUR SHOP?!
FWT!
FWT!
FWT!

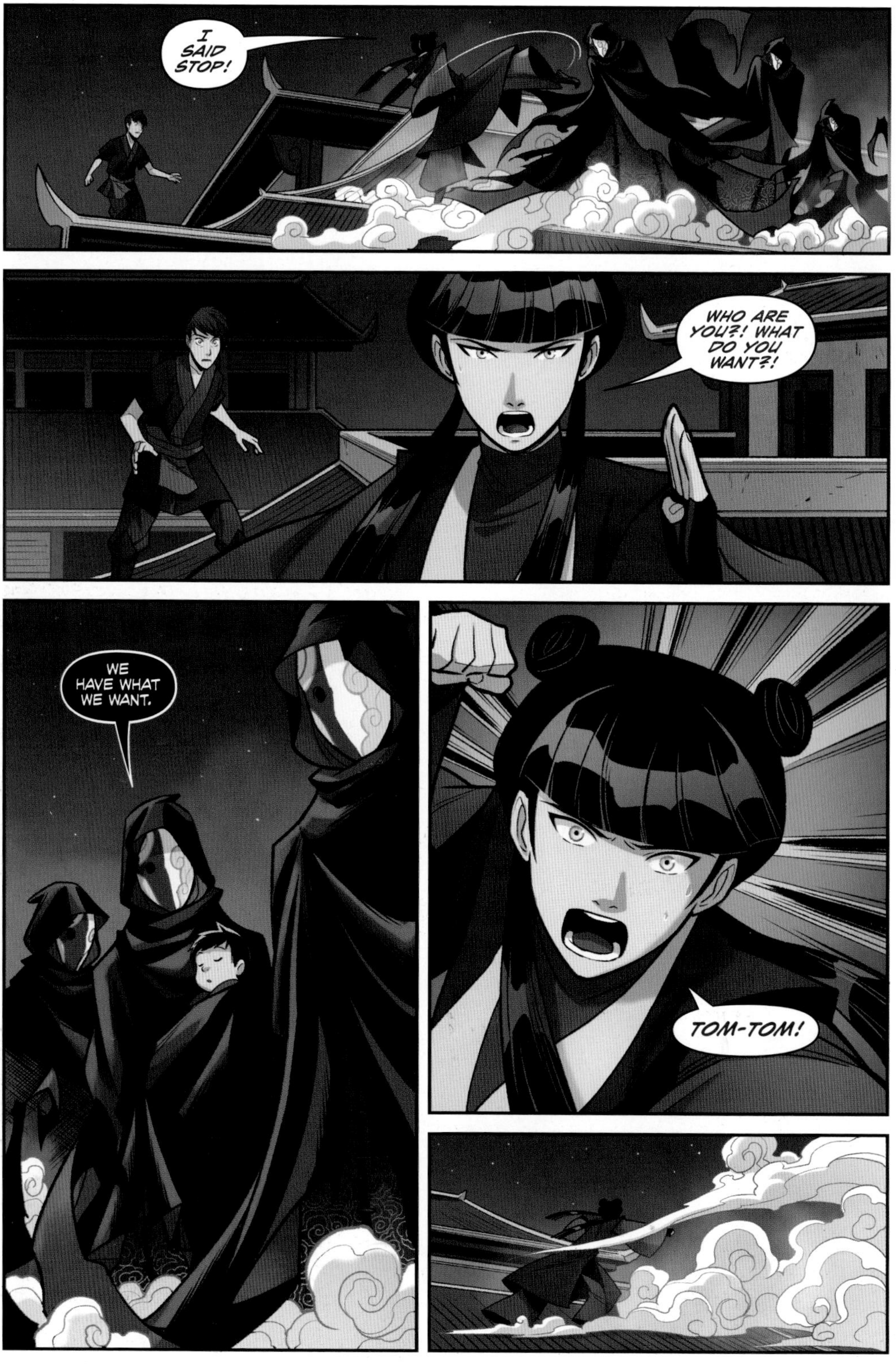
I SAID STOP!
WHO ARE YOU?! WHAT DO YOU WANT?!
WE HAVE WHAT WE WANT.
TOM-TOM!

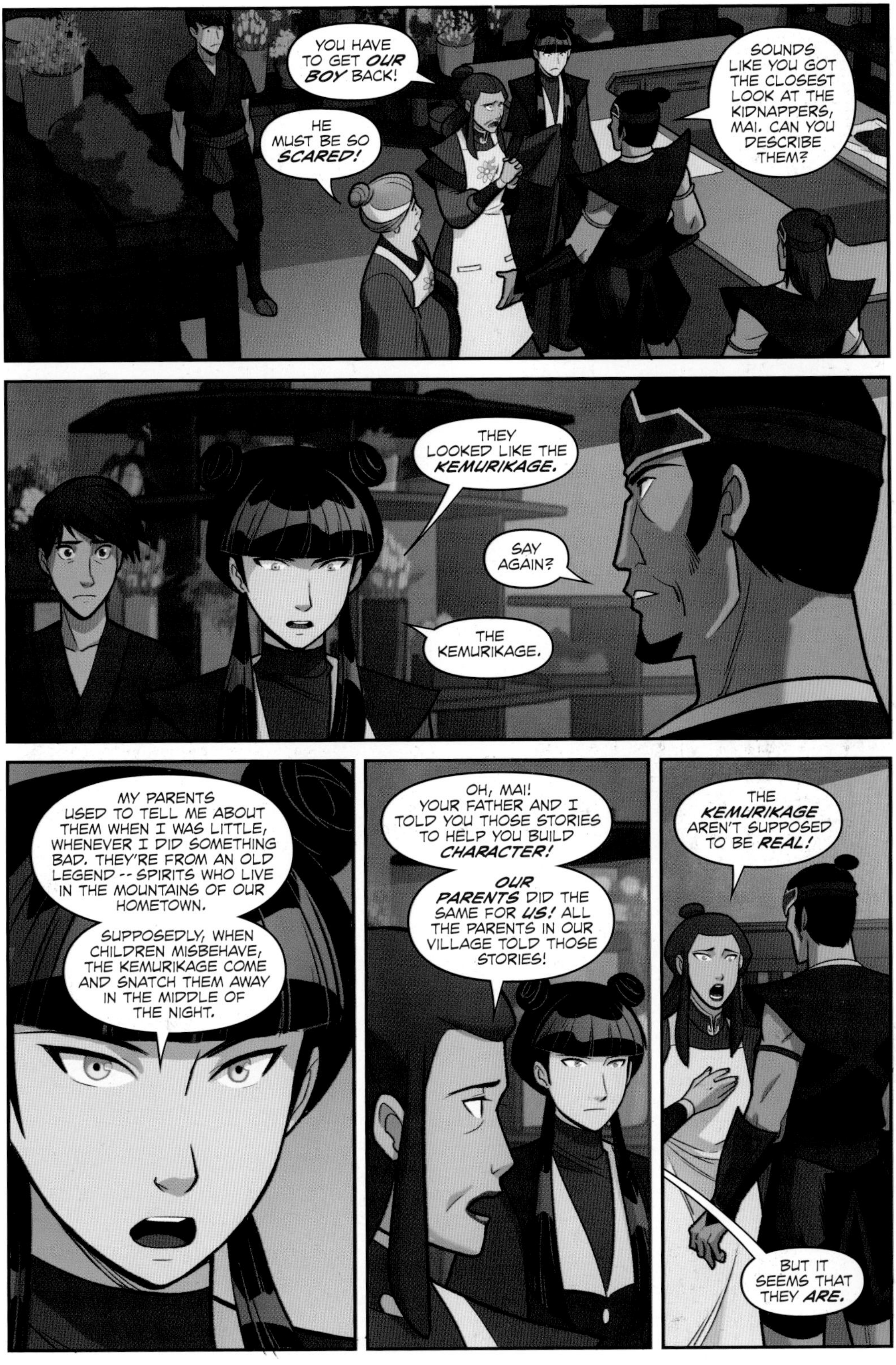
YOU HAVE TO GET OUR BOY BACK!
HE MUST BE SO SCARED!
SOUNDS LIKE YOU GOT THE CLOSEST LOOK AT THE KIDNAPPERS, MAI. CAN YOU DESCRIBE THEM?
THEY LOOKED LIKE THE KEMURIKAGE.
SAY AGAIN?
THE KEMURIKAGE.
MY PARENTS USED TO TELL ME ABOUT THEM WHEN I WAS LITTLE, WHENEVER I DID SOMETHING BAD. THEY'RE FROM AN OLD LEGEND -- SPIRITS WHO LIVE IN THE MOUNTAINS OF OUR HOMETOWN.
SUPPOSEDLY, WHEN CHILDREN MISBEHAVE, THE KEMURIKAGE COME AND SNATCH THEM AWAY IN THE MIDDLE OF THE NIGHT.
OH, MAI! YOUR FATHER AND I TOLD YOU THOSE STORIES TO HELP YOU BUILD CHARACTER!
OUR PARENTS DID THE SAME FOR US! ALL THE PARENTS IN OUR VILLAGE TOLD THOSE STORIES!
THE KEMURIKAGE AREN'T SUPPOSED TO BE REAL!
BUT IT SEEMS THAT THEY ARE.

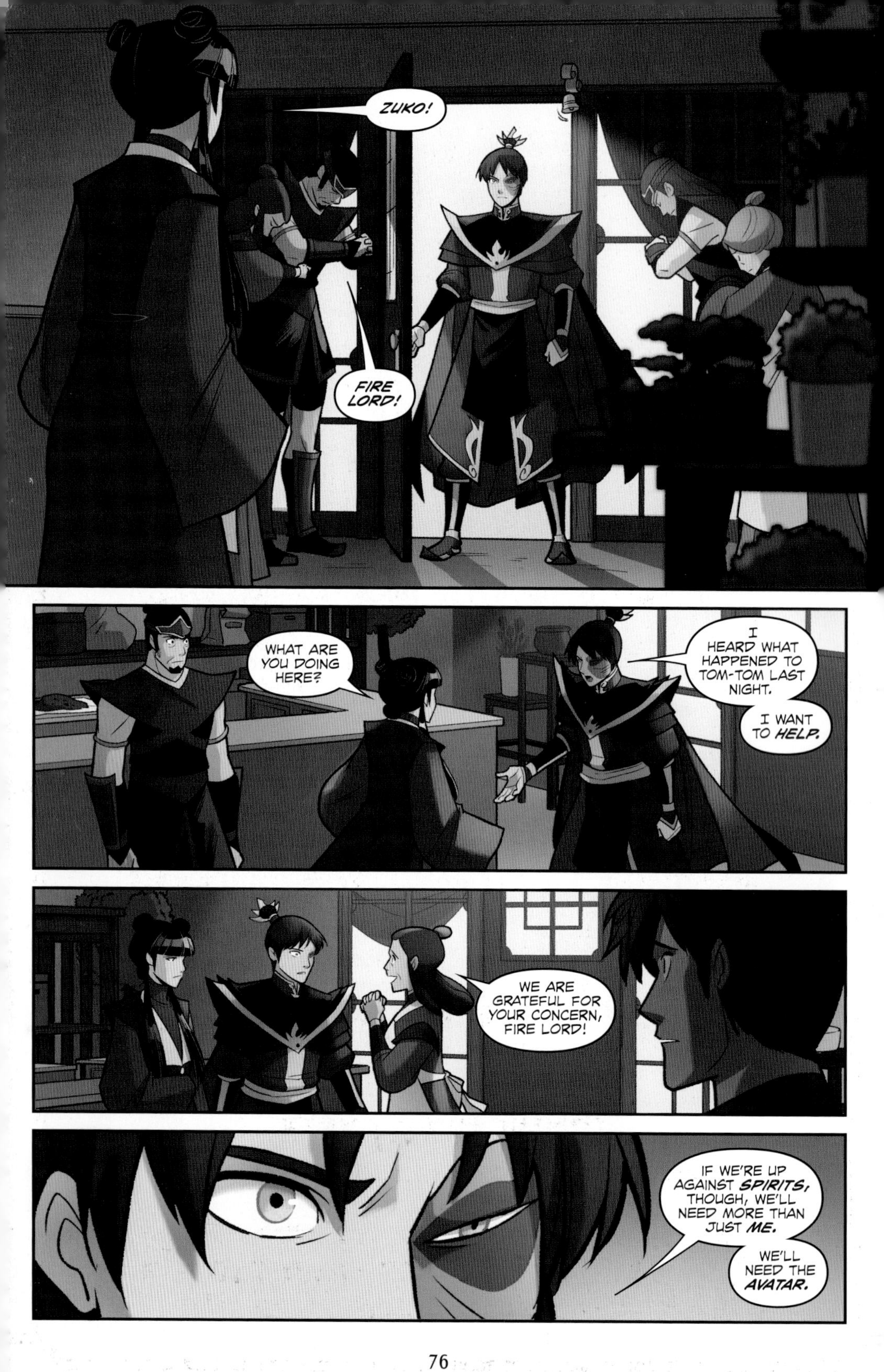
ZUKO!
FIRE LORD!
WHAT ARE YOU DOING HERE?
I HEARD WHAT HAPPENED TO TOM-TOM LAST NIGHT.
I WANT TO HELP.
WE ARE GRATEFUL FOR YOUR CONCERN, FIRE LORD!
IF WE'RE UP AGAINST SPIRITS, THOUGH, WE'LL NEED MORE THAN JUST ME.
WE'LL NEED THE AVATAR.

COMING IN DECEMBER

Aang and Zuko uncover the secrets of the Kemurikage in . . .

SMOKE AND SHADOW · PART TWO

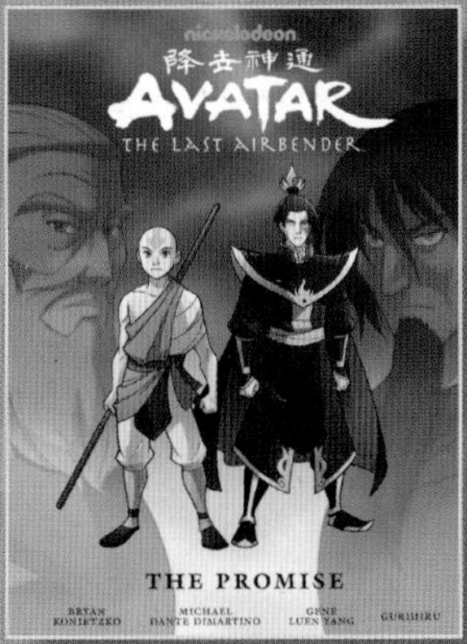
nickelodeon
降世神通
AVATAR
THE LAST AIRBENDER
THE PROMISE
BRYAN KONIETZKO
MICHAEL DANTE DIMARTINO
GENE LUEN YANG
GURIHIRU

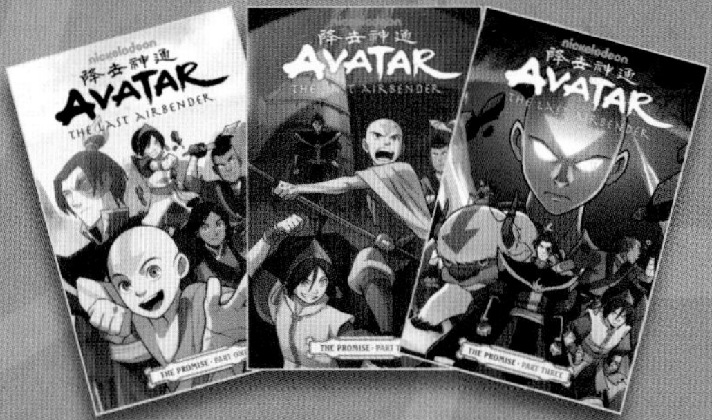
nickelodeon
降世神通
AVATAR
THE LAST AIRBENDER

Avatar: The Last Airbender—The Promise Library Edition
978-1-61655-074-5 $39.99

Avatar: The Last Airbender—The Promise Part 1
978-1-59582-811-8 $10.99

Avatar: The Last Airbender—The Promise Part 2
978-1-59582-875-0 $10.99

Avatar: The Last Airbender—The Promise Part 3
978-1-59582-941-2 $10.99

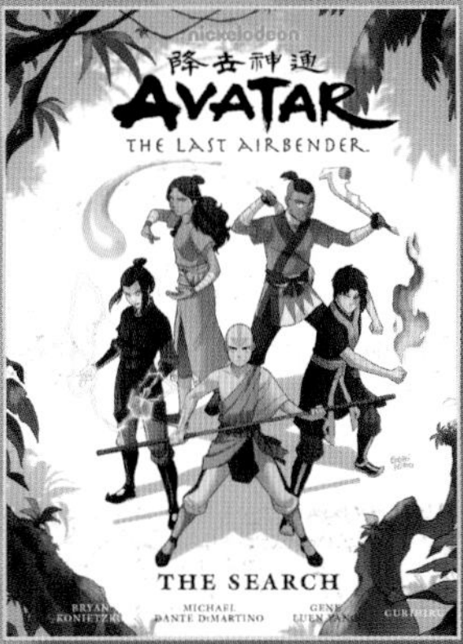
nickelodeon
降世神通
AVATAR
THE LAST AIRBENDER
THE SEARCH
BRYAN KONIETZKO
MICHAEL DANTE DIMARTINO
GENE LUEN YANG
GURIHIRU

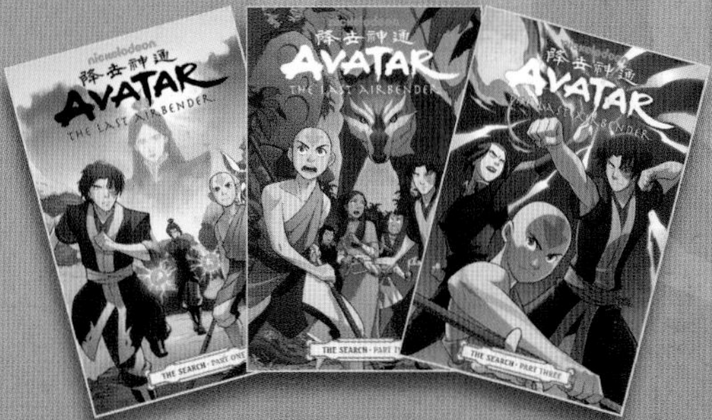
nickelodeon
降世神通
AVATAR
THE LAST AIRBENDER

Avatar: The Last Airbender—The Search Library Edition
978-1-61655-226-8 $39.99

Avatar: The Last Airbender—The Search Part 1
978-1-61655-054-7 $10.99

Avatar: The Last Airbender—The Search Part 2
978-1-61655-190-2 $10.99

Avatar: The Last Airbender—The Search Part 3
978-1-61655-184-1 $10.99

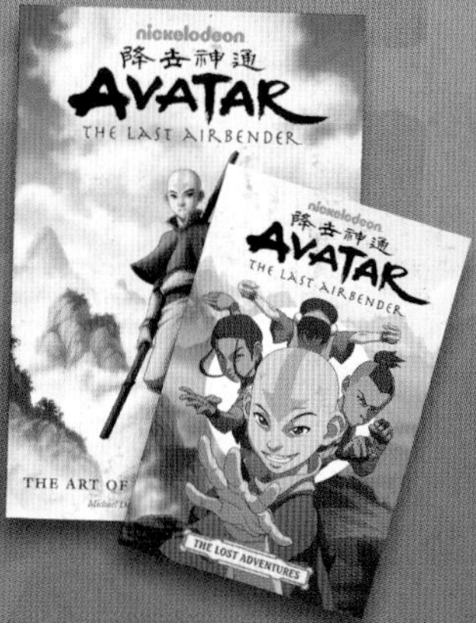
nickelodeon
降世神通
AVATAR
THE LAST AIRBENDER
THE LOST ADVENTURES

Avatar: The Last Airbender—The Art of the Animated Series
978-1-59582-504-9 $34.99

Avatar: The Last Airbender—The Lost Adventures
978-1-59582-748-7 $14.99

AVAILABLE AT YOUR LOCAL COMICS SHOP OR BOOKSTORE.

To find a comics shop in your area, call 1-888-266-4226

For more information or to order direct, visit DarkHorse.com or call 1-800-862-0052

DARK HORSE BOOKS

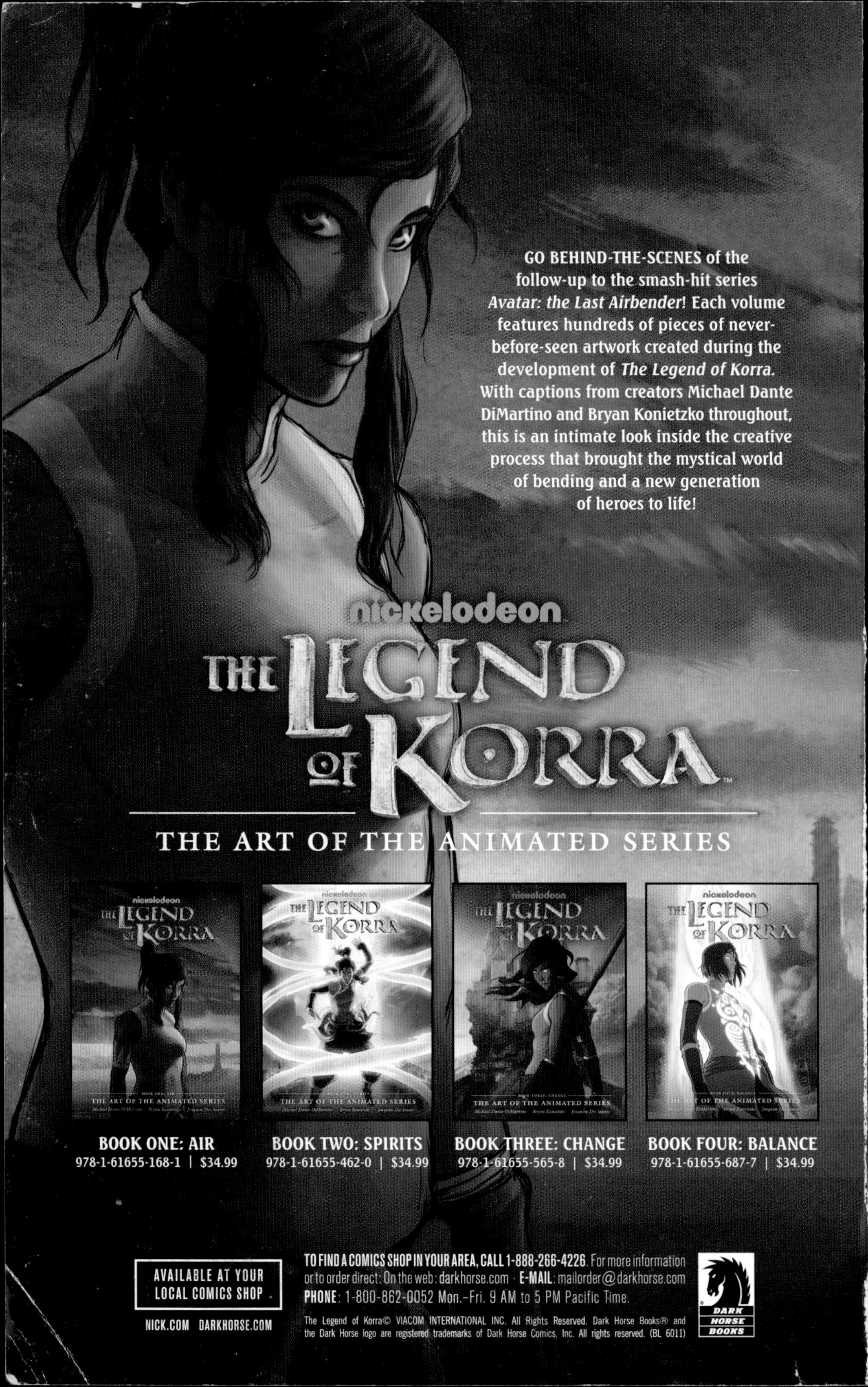
GO BEHIND-THE-SCENES of the follow-up to the smash-hit series *Avatar: the Last Airbender*! Each volume features hundreds of pieces of never-before-seen artwork created during the development of *The Legend of Korra.* With captions from creators Michael Dante DiMartino and Bryan Konietzko throughout, this is an intimate look inside the creative process that brought the mystical world of bending and a new generation of heroes to life!
nickelodeon
THE LEGEND OF KORRA™
THE ART OF THE ANIMATED SERIES
BOOK ONE: AIR
978-1-61655-168-1 | $34.99
BOOK TWO: SPIRITS
978-1-61655-462-0 | $34.99
BOOK THREE: CHANGE
978-1-61655-565-8 | $34.99
BOOK FOUR: BALANCE
978-1-61655-687-7 | $34.99
AVAILABLE AT YOUR LOCAL COMICS SHOP
NICK.COM DARKHORSE.COM
TO FIND A COMICS SHOP IN YOUR AREA, CALL 1-888-266-4226. For more information or to order direct: On the web: darkhorse.com · E-MAIL: mailorder@darkhorse.com
PHONE: 1-800-862-0052 Mon.-Fri. 9 AM to 5 PM Pacific Time.
The Legend of Korra© VIACOM INTERNATIONAL INC. All Rights Reserved. Dark Horse Books® and the Dark Horse logo are registered trademarks of Dark Horse Comics, Inc. All rights reserved. (BL 6011)
DARK HORSE BOOKS